To my parents

who have always been

a source of inspiration and guidance for me.

THE QURAN AND MANAGEMENT OF FAMILY RELATIONS

FOR EDUCATED YOUTHS

AFTAB ALAM KHAN

Made with ♥ on the Notion Press Platform
www.notionpress.com

Contents

Foreword

The Qur'an

and

Management of

Family Relations

By

Aftab Alam Khan

(M.Sc., CAIIB, Dip in HRD)

(Ex Senior Manager and Faculty Bank of Maharashtra)

Preface

In the name of God the Most Beneficent, the Most Merciful

All praise is due to God the Lord of the universe, the Beneficent the Merciful; Lord of the Day of Judgment. At the outset, I would like to thank the gracious God who has provided me an opportunity to use my insights about the Qur'an to write a book on a vital topic relating to family relations. I have titled the book "The Qur'an and Management of family Relations."

Initially, I had planned to write an article, but as I studied various verses of Qur'an on the topic, I realized that an essay would be inadequate. The Qur'an has covered this topic so elaborately and deeply that I decided to deal with the subject more deeply. This ambition motivated me to write an elaborate book, I have confined my study to the Holy Qur'an and have avoided lengthy academic discussions. I have mainly used the Qur'an and avoided secondary academic material.

Today, the institution of family is passing through great turmoil. The entire crisis has acquired unprecedented proportions. Never before in human civilization has the dignity and sanctity of this basic unit of society faced such challenges. The old joint family system that exercised effective control over its members is slowly disappearing.

It has given place to nuclear families, mainly comprising a husband; a wife and a few children. Today even this social unit is threatened with disintegration.

Due to the weakening of social control and the growth of liberal thinking, the divorce rate has increased worldwide. Often people approach courts for divorce on flimsy grounds. There are cases when the spouses simply desert the family for good and start leading independent lives without recourse to the courts. The level of tolerance and forbearance has fallen down quite low. This dangerous trend must be wisely reformed if we want to protect society from further downfall.

Another change we witness today is the trend of late marriages, single motherhood, man-women live-in-relationships, homosexuality and lax sexual relations. All these developments are detrimental to any society.

I firmly believe that Almighty God the Creator must have provided suitable guidance for us to lead a peaceful and prosperous life in His Book. While studying the Qur'an from this perspective, I noticed that many verses offer valuable advice for regulating family. I collected these verses, referred to commentaries of some eminent scholars and then formulated my thoughts. The more I worked on the subject, the more convinced I got that Almighty God had provided a handy and easily adaptable solution to various problems challenging humanity.

Here is an attempt to present various verses of the Qur'an on relevant topics, along with explanatory notes. I included multiple topics: husband-wife relationships, parent-child relationships, marriage and divorce, inheritance of property, nursing of children and orphans, and social evils like intoxication, gambling, adultery, etc. Some topics like Hijab and dress code are also included as they are also related to managing family life.

I have mainly used the English translation of the Qur'an by Maulana Waheeduddin Khan in this book. I have great respect for him as a great Islamic scholar. In some places, I have referred to the translation by Mohammad Asad and Maulana Abul Ala Maududi..

I offer my thanks to my mentor Late Jb. Ghafoor Parekh, the founder of Quranic Arabic Classes at Nagpur who had been kind enough to spare his valuable time to go through the script and offered valuable suggestions which were incorporated in the book. May Almighty God bless him with Rahmat and the Paradise. I am deeply indebted to my friends Dr. Sharfuddin Sahil and Dr. Mohammad Yusuf for their valuable suggestions in finalizing the manuscript of this book. I can't adequately thank my friend Dr Moin Qazi for transforming the contents into a finely produced book.

May God forgive me for all my shortcomings and weaknesses. It is just an honest attempt to bring ordinary people close to the teachings of the Qur'an so that they may be able to solve their problems in the light of the Holy Quran. May God accept this humble effort and provide salvation to me. I shall be very thankful to readers if they offer suggestions to improve the content and quality of this book.

Date : 11/12/2022

CHAPTER ONE

1. An introduction to the Quran

The Qur'an is the last and final version of divine guidance for humanity, also called the Word of God. The Most Merciful God revealed it through the Honoured Angel Gabriel to His last Prophet Muhammad (peace be upon him). It was not given to him by God in the form of a complete book as we see it today but was sent down in small parts, comprising a few verses and sometimes an entire chapter. The complete Qur'an was revealed to him over a period of 23 years of his prophet hood.

The Qur'an can rightly be called the True Book of Wisdom. It gives detailed knowledge about the heavens, the earth and all that exists between them. It rejects blind faith and appeals to people to use their intelligence to understand God has repeatedly asked people to think over His various creations; the Sun, the Moon and the stars in heaven, the mountains, the rivers and the oceans on the earth. In many places, God has asked people to count his blessings in the form of fruits, vegetables, cattle, fish, milk, honey, etc. He has invited our attention to the system of day and night, rains and winds, summer and winter, so that we can understand the greatness of God.

The first revelation was brought to him through the Angel Gabriel in 610 AD when Prophet Muhammad was in the Hira cave near Mecca He used to go there for prayer and meditation before he was appointed the Messenger of Allah but afterward he discontinued visiting Hira cave. The process of revelation of Quran continued for twenty three years and the final revelation came in 632 AD when the Prophet (Pbuh) was in Medina.

There are 114 chapters in Qur'an, and the verses number around 6353. The Qur'an was divided into 30 parts to meet the need of recitation. These 114 chapters that we find in the Qur'an are not arranged chronologically as per their revelations but were finally set in the present sequence, under the divine guidance through Angel Gabriel during the last year of the life of Prophet Muhammad (pbuh).

How was the Holy Qur'an Preserved?

When the Qur'an was revealed in the first quarter of the seventh century, the paper had already been invented, although in crude form. So, whenever any portion of the Qur'an was revealed, Prophet Muhammad would dictate it to one of his companions, from whom others would copy. Moreover, as the recitation of Quranic verses was an indispensable part of the regular prayers, several people simultaneously memorized the verses by heart. This process of dictation and memorization continued during the life time of the Prophet (Pbuh). Even after the demise of Prophet (pbuh), people continued this process of copying and memorization. Those who can memorize the whole Qur'an are called Huffaz (Singular-Hafiz).

During the caliphate of Hazrat Uthman bin Affan, when the Muslim rule had expanded to a more significant part of West Asia, a standard copy of the Qur'an was compiled by a board of companions of the Prophet. Then, several handwritten documents of this classic version of the Qur'an were prepared and sent to different cities within the caliphate. These copies were kept in the major mosques for people to recite and prepare documents.

Because of the increasing demand for the Quran, several people joined this work as a noble profession. They put in their best to prepare beautiful copies of the Quran. As a result, the art of Quranic calligraphy also developed. Quranic manuscripts in beautiful scripts and styles came into existence, preserved even today, in many museums in various parts of the world. When the printing press was invented, machines took up this work more efficiently. Today, we can get beautiful copies of the Qur'an worldwide without even the slightest variation.

Although the Qur'an was revealed in Arabic for the guidance of humanity, its authentic translations are available now in all the world's major languages. With the advancement of Information Technology, access to the Qur'an and its various translations and commentaries is at our fingertips through the internet. There are several websites available on the internet where we can read, listen and even download Qur'an on our computers and mobiles. This is a great blessing from Almighty God.

- **Selection from Holy Quran**

Here we have a few verses selected from the Holy Qur'an on different subjects to put before the readers an outline of the Holy book.

i) The first revelation of The Quran:

"Read in the name of thy Sustainer, Who has created. He created man out of a germ cell. Read, for thy sustainer is the Most Bountiful One, Who has taught (man) the use of the pen, He taught man what he did not know. (Qur'an - 96 : 1-5)

ii) The last revelation:

"And be conscious of the Day on which you shall be brought back unto God, whereupon every human being shall be repaid in full for what he has earned, and none shall be wronged." (Quran-2 : 281)

iii) Qur'an, the book of guidance for the Mankind:

"This Qur'an is an exposition for the people and a guidance and admonition for those who fear God." (Quran-3 : 138)

"O mankind there has come to you an admonition from your Lord, a cure for what is in the hearts (spiritual ailments) and a guide and blessing to the true believers." Quran-10 : 57

iv) The Power of Qur'an :

"Had we sent down Qur'an upon a mountain, you would certainly see it breaking into small pieces because of fear of God. We set forth these parables to men so that they may think over them. Quran-59 :21

v) The challenge of Quran to Mankind:

"If you are in doubt about the revelation that We have sent down to Our servant (Prophet Muhammad), then produce a single chapter like it, and call upon those who can help you beside God, if you are truthful.

(Quran-2:23)

vi) When was Qur'an Revealed?

"Ramazan is the month, when Qur'an was sent down as the guidance for mankind. It contains clear statements of guidance and the criterion by which to distinguish right

from wrong. Quran-2 : 185

vii) Allah has promised to protect Quran:

"It is We, Who have sent down the Reminder (Quran) and We will surely safe guard it. Qur'an 15:9

viii) Qur'an is for the benefit of mankind:

"We have explained clearly various examples for the benefit of mankind but man contradicts most of the things." Qur'an 18:54

ix) Qur'an is easy to understand:

"We have made it easy to learn lesson from the Quran. So, is there anyone who would learn lesson?"

(Qur'an 54:17)

"We have made this Qur'an easy to understand in your own language, so that they may learn lesson." Qur'an 44:54

x) People should deeply Think over Quran:

"This is a blessed book which we have sent down to you (Muhammad) for people to think over its messages and those with wisdom should learn lesson." Qur'an 38:29

"So, will they not reflect over this Quran? Or there are locks upon their hearts."

Qur'an 47:24

====================================

CHAPTER TWO

2. *The Objectives of the Quran*

Every book has its objective, and the Qur'an aims to provide proper guidance to humanity for making their lives successful in the present world and in the next world that is to come after death which is called the Hereafter. The Qur'an is a book of universal guidance for humanity. Everyone can draw guidance from it, Muslims and non-Muslims, farmers and businessmen, professionals and scholars, servants and masters, etc.

The Holy Qur'an contains all the topics and divine guidance necessary for the success of human beings in this world and the Hereafter. There are several verses in Qur'an which directly address to Mankind, believers, nonbelievers, Jews and Christians. So we all must study this book of wisdom regularly and reflect on its verses. The more we read this book, the more knowledge and jewels of wisdom we are able to glean from it.

Fundamental Teachings of the Quran:

It is better to know fundamental teachings of the Qur'an before we study different verses and draw conclusions from them. The Holy Qur'an mainly deals with the following subjects:

- **Monotheism:**

There is no God but Allah, the Creator and the Master of the Universe. He is One. No one is equal to Him. He is neither father nor son of anyone. He is Everlasting, He has no needs. No eye can see Him, but He can see all. He is the Master of life and death. Nothing happens in this world without His permission and consent. He alone should be worshipped without associating anyone with His power. All our invocations and supplications should be addressed to Him.

- **Belief in the life after death:**

Present world comprising all living and non-living things has a definite time period after that, it will come to an end. That day is called the Day of Qayamat. Allah has not revealed its time to anybody. It will happen suddenly. After some time, He will again create this world, raise all men and women to life, and evaluate the deeds they did in their past lives. This is called the Day of Judgment. Successful people will be blessed with the eternal happiness of Paradise, and those who are unsuccessful will be sent to Hell forever to undergo punishment for their misdeeds.

- **Belief in the prophethood:**

For the guidance of humanity Almighty God has sent many Messengers in various parts of the world since the time of Prophet Adam. They conveyed the teachings of God to the people of their times and presented the best role model before them. The names of twenty-six messengers and their instructions are mentioned in the Quran, but there were many more whose names are not mentioned. Some of the Messengers of God were provided with the Holy Books for the guidance of their people, but most of the Messengers of God were provided only with divine revelations. The principle teachings of all of them revolved around monotheism, the belief in life after death and the revelations of Almighty God.

List of prohibited and permissible items:

In the Qur'an we find a list of items that are prohibited for Muslims. Allah has not given this authority to anyone else including His Messengers. It is also mentioned in the Qur'an that all good things are permitted except those prohibited by the Lord. Various verses in the Qur'an deal with the dos and don'ts, items of virtues and sins, and right and wrong so that people may follow the right path.

- **Qur'an is the last divine book for the guidance of people**

The Qur'an is a book of divine instructions, warnings and good tidings. It defines God and His attributes; it contains stories of earlier generations and various Messengers of God. It is a book of knowledge that tells us many things we do not know.

The Qur'an provides answers to various questions that stir the human mind. Who is God and what are His attributes? Who is man and how did he come to earth? Who has created human and what is the purpose of his life? Who has created this whole universe and who controls it? Who has provided this life support system that caters to the needs of all living beings?

All these questions seek answers, and God has provided answers to these questions in His book, the Quran. This book of God profoundly impacted the lives of the people who first heard its message directly from Prophet (Pbuh) and who are called the companions of the Prophet and then, through them, the generations that followed them.

This Qur'an generated a spirit of intellectual curiosity and independent thinking that revolutionized the lives of its followers. Those who read this book cannot remain unaffected by its powerful impact. After all it is the word of Almighty God. Recitation of verses of Qur'an is obligatory in regular prayers (Namaz). Muslims are also asked to read and reflect over the verses of Qur'an during the day and night as much as they can. This is the book on whose basis the deeds of human beings will be judged and they will be rewarded or punished.

===

CHAPTER THREE

3. Family: the Basic Unit of Islamic Society

Man is never alone; he is born in society, lives in the community and dies in society. When he is born, he is so weak and dependent that he cannot survive even for a few hours if not properly cared for. For this reason, God has designed a system to take care of the child in the form of his mother, father, and other family members. He needs an exceptionally long time for his nursing to stand on his feet compared to other animals. He takes around 18 – 20 years to be an adult and take responsibility for his life.

All along his life, he is surrounded and supported by members of his family and society. When he is married, many people witness the event, and when he dies again, there are many near and dear to say goodbye to him. Family bonds are so strong that they do not dissolve even with death. His relatives and friends continue to remember him occasionally. They visit his grave and tomb and pray for him long after he has left the world.

- **The family relations are the strongest social bonds**

Members of the society are tied together by various bonds like family relations, caste, religion, race, language and profession, but the strongest of all the social bonds is the family bond. Family is the basic unit of society and typically consists of parents and their children. Sociologists call such a family a nuclear family. However, there may be extended families comprising the nuclear family and some other relatives like grandparents, uncles and aunts. Similarly, when two or more nuclear families live together in a single household and have a shared kitchen, they are called a joint family.

- **Strong family builds string society**

Family plays a vital role in a person's life and society's composition. **If the families are strong and supportive, society becomes strong; if the families are weak, society becomes weak.** Typically, a family fulfills the need of procreation, emotional needs, social needs, economic needs, and educational needs. So, when a family breaks down all these needs are affected and many problems arise. Unfortunately, during the last few decades, social bonds are weakened; as a result, divorces, failed marriages, domestic violence, property disputes, problems of orphans and old age parents have increased. There are other problems like the trend of late marriages, no marriage, no children, single motherhood, live-in-relationship, homosexuality, etc. Almighty God has provided detailed guidance on various subjects in His Holy Book. We would like to study divine guidance in the light of Quranic verses and find proper solutions for our problems.

- **Show kindness to parents**

Parent-child relation is the most important bond of family relation. It is the base on which the whole edifice of the family rests. If this bond is weakened, the foundation of the family institution will crumble.

"We have urged the man to show kindness to his parents. His mother has suffered many pains when he was in the womb; and in his breastfeeding for two years. So, be thankful to your parents and Me, and all will return to Me." (Qur'an: 31:14)

In the verse mentioned above, God has asked us to be kind and thankful to our parents. He reminds us to think about the pains a mother has to undergo during her pregnancy and the nursing of her baby. We can never repay them fully despite our best efforts, but we should always try to take care for them as much as possible specially when they are old.

-

Obey your parents

"But if they (parents) compel you to associate someone with Me, for which there is no reason, then do not obey them. Yet, be kind to them in this world and follow the path of those who turn to Me in devotion. Eventually, you will all return to Me, and I will tell you all that you have done." (Qur'an 31: 14-15)

We should be kind to our parents and obey them but if they ask you to make partners to Allah for then you should politely refuse it. Otherwise, you should obey them and be kind and dutiful to them in all worldly affairs. The family institution is so important that God wants to preserve and protect it even when there is a clash of religious beliefs.

•

Pray for Your Family:

'O' my Lord, make me and my children regular in prayer and accept my prayer. 'Oh Lord, forgive me and forgive my parents and all the believers on the Day of Reckoning (Day of Judgment)". (Qur'an 14: 40- 41)

This is a small prayer that Muslims offer after their regular prayer. They are asked to pray to God not only for their children and parents but also for the believers in general. This implies that believers should not have any grudge against anyone in the society and they should pray to God for their wellbeing and forgiveness.

•

Take special care of old parents:

"Your Lord has commanded that you should worship none but Him; and show kindness to parents. If either or both of them attain old age and they are with you, say no word of contempt to them, and do not rebuke them, but always speak gently to them, and treat them with humility and tenderness and say, 'Lord, be merciful to them both, as they raised me when I was little one. (Qur'an 17-23) In the verse mentioned above, God has given clear instructions to each individual on how to treat his parents, mainly when they are old and physically weak. He directed people to be kind and polite to their parents and should not rebuke them or hurt their feelings. They should serve them with love and humility and pray to God to be merciful to them.

- ### *Pray for Spouse and children:*

"And those who pray, "Our Lord grant us spouses and children, who will be the comfort of our eyes, and make us the leader of the righteous people." (Qur'an 25:74)

The above verse is a prayer of a true believer. A believer knows that nothing is possible without the blessings of God. Therefore, when he plans for marriage, he prays to Almighty God to bless him with a virtuous life partner who can make his life happy and blissful. Similarly, he prays to God for good children so that he may be happy in the life.

- ### *Infanticide is prohibited*

Do not kill children for fear of poverty and do not kill your children for fear of livelihood. We will provide for them and you. Indeed it is a great sin to kill them." (Qur'an 17 :31)

In verse mentioned above, there is an order from Almighty God not to kill your children for want of livelihood and poverty. God has promised to provide livelihood to all living beings so why He will not provide to you. So, he should have faith in God, be patient and continue his efforts for livelihood. Killing your babies also includes abortions without valid reasons which are illegal as per our laws also.

Thus from the above verses of the Quran, we learn that we must be kind and obedient to our parents. If we find some of their orders unjust, we can politely refuse them, but we should not offend their sentiments. We should take special care of them when they are old and dependent. We should always be thankful to God for His blessings, and we should also be grateful to our parents for their kindness. We should pray to God to bless us with good spouses and children. Lastly, we should never try resort to infanticide for want of subsistence as Almighty God has promised to provide livelihood to all living beings. In this way we will be able to form strong families and strong society.

==================================

CHAPTER FOUR

4. *Origin of Human*

Origin of man has been an enigmatic and difficult problem for the thinkers and philosophers. There are various views, beliefs, and theories about the origin of man. Hindus believe that man originated from the Brahma or Manu. Jews, Christians, and Muslims believe that the Almighty God created the first man Prophet Adam. Others do not believe in God. They say a man is the result of organic evolution, as mentioned in Darwin's theory of evolution, during the span of millions of years, without any intervention from God. Here we would like to present a few verses of Quran to learn the Quranic view.

- **Creation of Adam:**

"Your Lord said to angles, I am about to create a human being out of clay; and when I have formed him fully and breathed My spirit into him, prostrate yourselves before him. (Qur'an 38 : 71-72)

The verse mentioned above contains an injunction of Almighty God to the angels about the first human that He planned to create. Hecreated man from clay and when he was fully developed, God breathed His spirit into him, so he became a living creature. God named him Adam. How exactly it was done and what were the constituents of clay are not revealed in the Quran. Only Omniscient God knows the details.

- **God appointed human as caliph in the earth.**

"When your Lord said to the angles, 'I am going to appoint a caliph in the earth, they said, 'will You appoint someone there (as caliph) who will cause corruption on it and shed blood, while we glorify You, with your praise and extol your holiness," God answered; surely I know that, which you do not know. (Quran- 2:30)

The above-quoted verse narrates the dialogue between God and angels before the creation of the first man. When the Lord of the Universe disclosed the plan of creation and appointment of the human being as caliph or ruler on the Earth, the angels expressed their doubt about them. They said that if humans were made the rulers of the earth, they would cause corruption and bloodshed in the world and that they were always there to praise and glorify the Almighty God. But All-Knowing God rejected their argument and said," **Surely I know that, which you do not know.**" And He proceeded with His plan.

After the creation of Adam, He blessed him with knowledge not given to the angels. God asked them to tell Him the names of particular things around them, but the Angels expressed their inability to answer. The wordings of the second dialogue are as under.

- **God blessed human with the knowledge**

"And He taught Adam all the names (of various things), then He placed them before the angles and asked, "Tell me their names if you can truly do. They replied, "Glory be to You, we have no knowledge except what You have taught us. You are the All knowing, the wise. Then he said, "O' Adam, tell them their names. When Adam had told them their names, God said to the angles, "Did I not tell you that I know secrets of the heavens and the earth, and I know what you reveal and what you conceal" Qur'an 2:31-33

The following vital points are mentioned in the above verse.

- God has blessed man with knowledge not provided to the angels.
- Angels did not know anything about the talent of Adam, hence expressed their doubt.
- The source of all knowledge is God; He has complete knowledge of everything visible and invisible, open and secret.

The verses mentioned above tell us, Almighty God created Adam from clay, and then He blessed him with knowledge and other abilities which He did not give to other creatures. Also, He appointed humans as caliphs or rulers on the earth in spite of objections from angels.

- **Creation of Eve:**

'O, Mankind! Be conscious of your Lord, Who created you from a single individual (Adam). He created his mate (Eve) from him, and from the two of them, spread countless men and woman. And remain conscious of God, in whose name you appeal to one another, and be mindful of your

obligations in respect of ties of kinship, God is always watchful over you.' (Qur'an 4:1)

The verse mentioned above deals with the creation of Mother Eve and the formation of the first family of human beings. The following points are covered in the above-quoted verse.

- "Be conscious of your Lord" means; we should know and understand the greatness and power of Almighty God. This we can do by reflecting on all the living and nonliving things around us.
- God created human society from a single individual Adam, subsequently, He appointed him His Messenger for the guidance of future generations.
- After the creation of Adam, God created a female partner from him, whom He named Eve. **This is how the first family came into existence.**
- Then, He created all human beings through reproduction. Thus we can infer that all human beings are children of Adam and Eve. They are all equal, and no one is higher or lower based on their family, cast and creed, place of birth, language and race.
- We should be mindful of our behavior with the blood relatives. There is specific instruction from our Lord about them and if we overlook it then we are answerable to God.
- God is watching us all the time so we are under His constant surveillance for whatever we do at night or during the day.

<u>Development of child in womb</u>

"We created man from an essence of clay, then We placed him as a drop of fluid in a safe place, then We

developed that drop into zygote, and then We developed that into embryo and We developed that embryo into bones, and clothed the bones with flesh. Then We brought him into being as a new creation. Glory be to God, the best of creators". (Qur'an: 23/12-14)

The verse mentioned above describes the biological details of development of baby in the womb of a mother. It starts from semen, and when a sperm enters into an egg of a woman in the uterus a zygote is formed, then zygote develops into an embryo that clings to the uterus. Then bones are developed and bones are covered with flesh and the baby takes the shape of a human baby. This is how the baby develops in the womb and finally comes in the world.

Creation of human race:

" (God asks) Who originates creation, then regenerates it, and who gives you sustenance from heaven and earth? So, is there a deity besides God?" Say, "Bring forward your proofs, if you are telling the truth." (Qur'an: 27/64)

Like all other living beings humans also grow through a process of reproduction, but in the human being the process of reproduction is highly regulated. There is a well defined set of norms, rules and traditions in every society which people have to follow if they want to form a family and have children. In the above verse God the most high presents three questions to the people about their creation, their regeneration and their sustenance and then asks "Is there a deity besides God"? The main purpose of this verse is to stir the mind of the people to think who they should worship.

=======================================

CHAPTER FIVE

5. History of the Satan

Human history is incomplete without understanding the personality of Satan. He is the chief instigator and the biggest enemy of man. His principle aim is to misguide human beings from the right path shown by Almighty God through instigations, deceptions and falsehood and lead them to the Hell. For this reason God has commanded believers to beware of Satan and pray to God and seek His shelter from the Satan. Here we quote a few verses from Qur'an about the Satan which will tell us about his aim and objectives and why he disobeyed the God.

- **God created Jinn from the flame of fire**

"He has created man from rotten clay and He has created the Jinn from the flame of fire." Qur'an 55: 14-15

The above-mentioned verses tell us that Human is created from rotten clay and Jinns are created from the flame of fire. Jinns are nonmaterial beings and hence are invisible to us but they remain all around us to misguide us from the right path. There are a lot of stories about Jinns but we shall confine ourselves to the verses of Qur'an.

- **Disobedience of Iblis**

"When We commanded the angels," Bow yourselves to Adam."All bowed but Iblis, he refused to do so; and acted proudly and became disobedient." (Qur'an 2: 34)

Before the creation of humans, angels and Iblis lived in the Heavens. Iblis is the name of the Jinn. When God created Adam He asked all of them to bow themselves to Adam. All the angels followed the order but Iblis defied and disobeyed and proudly refused to bow to Adam. The actual dialogue is mentioned in the below-mentioned verses.

"When we said to angles,' Bow down to Adam, they all bowed down except Iblis, he said,' Am I to bow down to someone you have created out of clay? And he further said, "Tell me, "Is this the being that you have exalted above me? If you reprieve me until the day of resurrection, I will bring all but a few of his descendents under my sway." (Qur'an:17: 61-62)

From the verses mentioned above we learn, when God commanded angels to bow down to Adam and accept the superiority of the newly created creature, all bowed down except Iblis who is also called the Satan. He argued with the Almighty God that as Adam was created from clay, he was superior to Adam, so he would not bow down to Adam. And he was so arrogant that, when his argument was rejected by God, instead of seeking pardon, he asked Almighty Lord to give him reprieve till the day of resurrection. He could overpower most people and prove that he was superior to man and more eligible to be the caliph of the earth. Because of this arrogance he was condemned by God in the following verses.

- **God condemns Iblis:**

"God said, 'The Hell shall be your reward and the reward of any of them who follow you; an ample recompense. Go ahead and entice whomsoever, you can with your voice; and mount assaults against them with your cavalry and infantry; and be their partner in wealth and children; and make promises to them. And the promise of the Satan is nothing but delusion. (God further said). But you shall have no power over my true servants; your Lord shall be their all sufficient Guardian. (Qur'an 17: 63-65)

The verses mentioned above in the Qur'an contain the following points.

- Satan was aware of the divine plan of man's stay over earth for a certain period. He was also aware that man would be required to follow the commands of God and those who follow them would be rewarded with Paradise, and the evil doers would be punished in Hell.
- The Merciful God not only granted Iblis reprieve till the day of resurrection but challenged him to use all his wisdom, power, resources and forces to misguide humanity. But God clarified that he would never overpower his faithful followers.
- Enticements and false promises are the two primary tools of Satan to mislead and misguide humanity. There is no doubt that God has granted him the freedom to use them against man.

- **Satan is enemy of humans:**

" O' believers surrender yourselves totally to God, and do not follow in the footsteps of Satan; surely, he is your sworn enemy. " **(Qur'an2:208)**

We must always keep in mind that Satan is our biggest enemy. He has pledged before God to mislead and misguide human from the right path by prompting them to be unfaithful and ungrateful, so whenever a negative thought comes in our mind we should be cautious.

- **Seek refuge of Allah from Satanic provocations:**

"If an evil impulse from Satan provokes you, seek refuge with God; He is all hearing, and all knowing.When any evil suggestion from Satan touches those who fear God, they are instantly alerted and become watchful." (Qur'an 7:200)

In the above verse Almighty God has asked us to be alert and seek His refuge whenever there is an evil impulse from Satan and take suitable measures to solve the problem.

- **On the Day of Judgment Satan would refuse to accept the blame:**

"When the Judgment has been passed, Satan will say to them, "God made you a true promise; I too made you promises, but I failed you. I had no authority over you, except that I called you and you responded to me. Do not now blame me, but blame yourselves! I cannot help you, nor can you help me. I reject your former act in associating me with God." The wrongdoers will have a painful punishment." (Qur'an: 14: 22)

The above verse makes it amply clear that Satan will not accept any blame for sending the wrongdoers to Hell; they will be fully responsible for their deeds and will face punishment.

Considering the above verses of the Quran, we can infer that Satan is man's biggest enemy. He never wants that man should ever succeed in this world and the Hereafter. He tries his best to misguide man, and put hurdles in the right path so that a maximum number of people may be condemned to Hell. Therefore we should always be alert lest we are misguided by Satan. Moreover, we should always pray to Almighty God to save us from the mischief and enticements of Satan.

======================================

CHAPTER SIX

6. *Arrival of Adam and Eve upon the Earth*

After the creation of Adam and Eve, God asked both of them to live in Paradise. He asked them to live peacefully and enjoy all types of fruit and drinks, but He warned them not to eat fruit from a particular tree; otherwise, they would be punished. Also, God cautioned them against their enemy Satan, to beware of his enticements and ruses. This is narrated in the verses mentioned below.

- **Satan tempted Adam and Eve to disobey God:**

" O Adam! You and your wife shall live in Paradise and eat and drink there, wherever you wish, but you shall not approach this tree, lest you shall be defaulters. But Satan tempted them so that he might expose their nakedness which had been hidden from them. He said, 'your Lord has forbidden you to approach this tree, lest you become angels or immortals. And he swore to them." I am in deed your well-wisher." Qur'an – 7: (19-21)

Initially they were cautious and took due care not to go near the forbidden tree but with the passage of time they forgot the warning and became complacent. Satan was waiting for this opportunity. He came to them as their well-wisher and tried to reason with them; if they ate the fruit from the prohibited tree, they would become angels and immortals and shall never die. But Adam and Eve did not believe him and ignored him. Satan continued his efforts to entice them, and ultimately succeeded in misleading them.

Some people believe that Satan convinced Mother Eve first, and then she persuaded Adam to eat the forbidden fruit. They believe that Mother Eve is the cause of the expulsion of humans from Paradise. But this presumption is not supported by the Qur'an. Further events are mentioned in the below-mentioned verses.

- **Adam and Eve seek forgiveness:**

"Thus he misguided them deceitfully. So when they both tasted the fruit of the tree, their nakedness was exposed, then they started covering themselves with the leaves of the Garden. Then their Lord called out to them 'Did I not forbid you to approach that tree, and did I not say to you that Satan was your declared enemy? They replied, "Our Lord, we have wronged to ourselves, and if you shall not forgive us, and have mercy upon us, we shall be losers. The God said, "Go down from here as enemies to each other. And for you there is an abode and provisions on earth for a period. There you shall live, there you shall die, and you shall be raised again from there." Qur'an 7 : 22-25

The verses contain the following points

- They were disrobed as soon as Adam and Eve ate the forbidden fruit. It also implies that after the creation of Adam and Eve, both were provided with clothes.
- When they were naked, they tried to cover themselves with the leaves of trees. This tells us that the feeling of

shame in a human being is inborn and natural and for this reason clothes are the indispensible part of human civilization.

- To make someone naked is a sort of punishment. And this punishment was awarded to them for their disobedience.
- Both Adam and Eve admitted their mistake and sought God's mercy and forgiveness. God forgave them both but asked all of them, including Iblis, to go down to Earth to spend the remaining period of their lives.

- Satan is the biggest enemy of man. He had vowed before God to mislead humanity and try his best to push them into the fire of Hell. So man should also consider Satan his enemy and should never befriend him. We should always seek refuge from Satan's evil designs from the Almighty Lord.

- The present life on earth has to end one day, called the Qayamat or Doomsday. After that, all human beings and Jinns would be raised again and presented before God. Their deeds would be evaluated, and they would be either rewarded with Paradise or punished in Hell. This is called the Day of Judgment or the Day of Evaluation. Belief in the Day of Judgment is one of the fundamental articles of faith for Muslims.

- **God sends Adam and Eve to Earth:**

"We said, 'Go down all of you from here; and when guidance comes to you from Me, those who follow my guidance will have no fear, nor will they grieve, and those who deny and reject our commands shall be the inhabitants

of the Hell. Therein they shall abide forever." (Qur'an 2:38-39)

Before sending Adam and Eve to earth Almighty God again advised them, "Henceforth earth would your place of residence. There you would be provided with guidance from time to time. If you follow the guidance properly you would be rewarded with the Paradise but if you disobeyed you would be sent to the Hell."

Today we have divine guidance in the form of Holy Quran. It's our duty to read this book and follow its commands to be successful in this world and in the Hereafter. Those who follow this divine book will have no fear and grief on the Day of Judgment, and those who deny and reject this book will reside in Hell forever. This is the true account of the journey of Adam and Eve from Paradise to earth.

==================================

CHAPTER SEVEN

7. The Islamic Charity and Relatives

Human society is always composed of haves and have-nots. There are some people who are rich and have surplus resources and there are others who are poor and destitute. This is as per the divine scheme. This is the reason, we find poverty not only in the poor and developing countries but also in the most developed and rich countries. Poverty is the root cause of many crimes. To fight this problem governments across the world conduct different poverty alleviation programmes which are mostly based on increasing the family income by providing them suitable employment and subsidies. Islam provides an additional channel in the form of charity to solve the problem of poverty and hunger. This is the reason we find a large number verses in Qur'an which provide elaborate guidance about compulsory and voluntary charity. They are referred as Zakat and Sadaqat. Some of the important verses are presented as under.

- **Charity is a great virtue:**

"Virtue does not consist in whether you face towards the East or the West; virtue means believing in God, the Last

Day, the angels, the Book and the prophets; the virtuous are those who, despite their love for it, give away their wealth to their relatives and to orphans and the very poor, and to travelers and those who ask [for charity], and to set slaves free, and who attend to their prayers and pay the alms, and who keep their pledges when they make them, and show patience in hardship and adversity, and in times of distress. Such are the true believers; and such are the God-fearing." (Qur'an: 2:177)

In the verse mentioned above Almighty God has defined ' Virtue'. They can be divided in two categories namely faith and practice. Faith includes belief in God, belief in the Last Day, belief in the angels, belief in all the Divine Books and belief in all the Messengers of God. Noble practices include various charity expenditures (Sadaqat), regular prayers, Zakat (Compulsory charity), honour pledges and show patience in hardships. Also we see that out of ten virtues two virtues come under charity category and it is described in detail. This reflects the importance of charity in Islam.

- **Expenditure over parents and Relatives:**

"They ask you what they should spend in charity, say, 'Whatever you spend should be for parents, close relatives, orphans, the needy and the wayfarers. God is well aware of whatever good you do." (Qur 2: 215)

In the verse mentioned above, God presented a list of people, who were eligible for financial support, but mentioned parents first, then relatives and others. We should try to follow this priority list in our charity works. Blood relatives have strong affinity and are closer to each other than other members of the society in happiness and sorrow; therefore they should be given top priority in charity.

- **Charity can be private or public:**

"If you give charity openly, it is good, but if you keep it secret and give to the needy in private, that is better for you, and it will atone for some of your bad deeds. God is aware of all that you do." (Qur'an: 2:271)

Charity can be given openly in public or privately, both are permitted and God has promised good return for them but if it is done privately it is better. Sometimes there is request for charity in public and sometimes people request it privately, so depending upon the situation it can be done. However charity should be for Allah and not for name and fame.

- **Loans can be written off as charity:**

"If the debtor is in difficulty, then grant him respite till a time of ease. If you were to write it off as an act of charity that would be better for you, if only you knew" (Qur'an: 2:280)

There are some who borrow loan from their relatives and friends but they are unable to repay as per their promise. In the above verse Allah has asked us to be considerate and give them respite. And if there is genuine problem, it would be better to treat it as charity. Thus charity helps greatly in building healthy social relations.

- **Poor have right over our resources:**

"Give relatives their due and also to the needy and the wayfarers (homeless). And do not spend extravagantly. Indeed spendthrifts are brothers of Satan, and Satan is ever ungrateful to his Lord. And if you are waiting for your Lord's bounty that is yet to come, and you have to turn them away, then speak to them politely." (Qur'an 17 : 26-28)

The above-quoted verse tells us that relatives, the poor, the homeless and other needy people have the right over our resources and we are commanded to help them voluntarily. If we do not follow this command we are likely to be punished for disobedience. The term wayfarer includes all those who are travelers in need, and those homeless people lying on roads. Secondly, we should not be spendthrift. Such people can hardly save anything to give in charity to others. Such people are called the brothers of Satan. Thirdly, If we do not have something to give to a beggar or needy person, we should decline him politely without hurting his feelings.

- **We are only the trustee of wealth that we have:**

"Have faith in God and His Messenger and spend in charity from that of which He has made you trustees: those of you who believe and give alms shall be richly rewarded." (Qur'an: 57: 7)

In this verse Allah the most high has clarified that we are only the trustee of the wealth that we have, Allah is the real owner. Also, there is command from Him to give alms and charity for which they will be richly rewarded.

- ***Miserliness and extravagance:***

"And do not be too miserly nor be too extravagant so that you become destitute and needy. Indeed your Lord gives abundantly to whomsoever He wants and limits to whom He wants. He is well informed and watchful of His servants." (Qur'an 17 : 29-30)

In the verse quoted above there is an instruction, neither be too miserly nor be extravagant, both are evils. We should exercise proper control over our expenditure. Secondly, our Lord provides wealth in abundance or in limit to whomsoever He wills so actually God is the real owner and we are only the trustee. Hence, we are responsible for spending the wealth judiciously as per the commands of God to whom we are accountable on the Day of Judgment.

From the verses mentioned above it is amply clear that Islam gives great importance to charity which helps us building strong family relations and other social relations, as a result a welfare society is formed.

==============================

CHAPTER EIGHT

8. Maintain Good Relations with People

Maintaining good social relations are very important for building a happy society. We have very close relationship with the members of our families, relatives and family friends but there are others who come in our contacts frequently, like neighbors, colleagues and subordinates. A healthy and welfare society is one where people voluntarily take care of each other and maintain good relationships. There are detailed instructions for us in the Holy Qur'an as under.

"And Worship God, and do not associate partners with Him. And be good to your parents, to relatives, to the orphans, to the needy; and to the neighbour who is your relative, and the neighbor who is not related to you; and to the companions by your side and the wayfarers, and those whom you rightfully possess (servants and staff). Surely, God does not like arrogant and boastful people." (Quran: 4 -36)

. In the verse quoted above we get comprehensive guidance on the topic but at the outset Almighty advised mankind about their relationship with Him. They should not worship anyone except God and should not associate anyone with Him. He is the Creator, the Sustainer and the

Lord of the universe. All our worship and prayers are due to Him. Other points are mentioned below.

- **Relationship with parents:**

After God parents are the most important persons for an individual. They have immense obligations over us. So God has asked us to be good to your parents. To be good to parent means we should behave with them respectfully, talk to them nicely, help them in their works, be obedient to them and lastly take special care of them when they become old.

- **Relationship with Relatives:**

After parents come relatives who play a very important role in the life of a person. This includes both blood relations and in-laws. Most of our social and cultural interactions are with this group. In the above verse God has asked us to maintain good relations with all of them. But this requires good qualities like tolerance, patience and sacrifice without which there is chance of spoiling the relations and peace of mind.

- **Orphans:**

Children who have lost their mother and father are the neediest persons so God has mentioned them just after relatives. It is the primary responsibility of the close blood relatives to take care of them. After them it is the collective responsibility of the society to take care of them till they reach the age of maturity.

- **Needy People:**

This includes poor, destitute and all other people who are victims of circumstances and misfortune. We should offer them financial and other support to fulfill their needs. Local mosques in the area can play an important role in identifying such needy persons and satisfying their needs.

- **Relationship with neighbors:**

Maintaining good relations with the neighbors is very important for living happy and peaceful life. They are physically closer to us and can help us in case of emergency. God has asked us to be good to them. We can adopt the same strategy to build up healthy relationship as we adopt for the relatives i. e. tolerance, patience and sacrifice. Otherwise they can become a permanent cause of nuisance for us and spoil our peace of mind.

- **Relationship with strangers:**

Sometimes we come in contact with people during journey or some social programmes. Even though they are strangers God has asked us to be good to them. We should behave them decently. Quite possible this casual meet results in deeper relation.

- **Relationship with staff and servants:**

We spend a lot of time with our colleagues, subordinates and servants in our business and profession. Healthy relations with them create a positive atmosphere for work which is beneficial for all. God has asked us to maintain good relations with them also. To keep pleasant smile on face, talk politely, exchange greetings and offer gifts on important occasions go a long way in building healthy social relations.

- **Don't be arrogant:**

In the last portion of the verse God has warned us against the evil of arrogance and boasting, for nobody likes such a person. Arrogance is the most negative quality that spoils social relations therefore we must discard it from our personality.

- **Speak kindly to People:**

" When We made a covenant with the Children of Israel, "Worship none but God and be good to your parents and to relatives and orphans and the needy. And speak kindly to people. Attend to your prayers and pay the zakat [prescribed alms]." But with the exception of a few, you turned away [in aversion] and paid no heed." (Qur'an: 2:83)

In the verse mentioned above first five points are common as mentioned in Qur'an:4: 36. Other points include speak kindly to people, and offer prayer and pay zakat. Our mutual relations depend upon the way we talk with our relatives and friends. If we talk to them nicely and treat them kindly we can develop strong relationship; on the contrary if we are rude and arrogant no one would like to associate with us. Jews were also asked to be regular in prayers and pay zakat but most of them did not follow the commands.

- **Follow the path of Justice, Kindness and Charity**

"God commands justice, kindness and giving to relatives, and He forbids all shameful deeds, and injustice and transgression. He admonishes you so that you may take heed!" (Qur'an:16:90)

Justice, kindness and charity play very important role in building healthy social relations, hence these commands. On the other hand shameful deeds, injustice and transgressions are big vices which destroy society therefore they are prohibited by God.

- **Avoid Social Evils**

Common social evils like consumption of liquor, drugs and gambling have powerful adverse impacts on family relations; therefore Almighty God has provided clear guidelines on these matters in the holy Qur'an.

"They ask you about intoxicants and gambling Say, "There is great sin in both; although they have some benefits for people, their harm is more significant than their benefit." (Qur'an 2:219)

In the verse mentioned above, Almighty God described all intoxicants as great sins. They include alcohol, marijuana (ganja), opium, drugs and other intoxicating materials and those who consume such intoxicants shall be punished. Likewise, gambling is also prohibited and is described as a great sin. Gambling includes all games of chances, playing cards, betting, lotteries, satta bazaar, etc. Although there are some profits but their losses outweigh their profits. This is evident from the lives of those addicted to gambling, drugs and liquor, their families are destroyed. It is also seen that most heinous crimes like murder, rape and physical assaults are committed under influence of liquor. Liquor is also the main cause of domestic violence and family break up. Often gambling becomes the cause of financial bankruptcy and mutual rivalry.

- **Relatives, Poor and wayfarers have right over our assets:**

"Give to your relatives their due, and also to the needy and the wayfarer. Yet do not spend extravagantly" (Qur'an: 17:26)

As our children and parents have right over our assets similarly relatives, poor and wayfarers too have some right over us. This is the most striking feature of Islamic charity. It is not just a virtuous deed and an act of kindness; it is our duty to help the relatives, poor and needy.

Thus these verses provide us detail guidance about how to develop good social relations and form a healthy and welfare society.

==================================

CHAPTER NINE

9. Promote Marriage in the Society

Family is essential building blocks for the construction of society and has crucial role in social development. Families bear the primary responsibility for education and socialization of children as well as instilling values of citizenship in the society. And marriage is an institution through which a family is formed. A simple ceremony of marriage converts a man into a husband and a woman into a wife. Both get a new set of relatives called as in-laws, and get license to produce children for the growth of society. Keeping in view its importance Almighty God has provided valuable guidance in His holy book the Qur'an.

"Marry those among you who are singles, and those of your male and female servants and subservient who are fit (for marriage). If they are poor, God will provide for them from His bounty, for God's bounty is infinite and He is all-knowing.

And those who do not have means to marry should keep themselves chaste until God grants them enough out of His bounty." (Qur'an 24 32-33

In the verses mentioned above, there are important instructions from Almighty God regarding marriage.

- Once children reach marriageable age, they should be married. This is an instruction from God. Marriage should not be delayed for long in search of ideal match. We should have a compromising attitude and finalize the matter without much delay.
- There is an instruction from God not to leave servants and subservient as single. Once they reach the marriageable age, they should also be counseled to get married. An unmarried man or women around you or your family is a potential threat. Satan may instigate them for evil.
- Sometimes poverty or weak financial position becomes the reason for delay in marriage. But this problem should not be magnified. No sooner there is reasonably comfortable position the marriage should be performed. It is not only a biological need but an important social responsibility without which human society cannot survive.
- To maintain virginity is another instruction of God to the people. They are advised to keep themselves chaste and should refrain from illegal sexual relations.

- **Adultery is prohibited:**

"And do not approach unlawful sexual intercourse. Indeed, it is extreme immorality and an evil way." (Qur'an 17:32)

Almighty God has prohibited all sorts of illegal sexual relationships whether with consent or without consent and has provided deterrent punishment for the crime. So we should keep away from it at all cost.

- **Punishment for adultery:-**

"This is a chapter that We have revealed (in Quran) and which We have made obligatory; We have sent down clear instructions in it so that you may take heed. Flog the adulteress and the adulterer, each of them with a hundred stripes. And let not compassion with them keep you from carrying out this law of God if you truly believe in God and the Last day; and let a group of the believers witness their punishment." (Qur'an 24:1-2)

Instructions in the above verses of the Qur'an are obligatory, meaning we must comply. Both men and women are to be punished for committing adultery. And the prescribed punishment is a hundred stripes to be awarded in public view. And believers are asked not to show any compassion at the time of punishment.

All the guidelines about dress code and Hijab in various verses in the Qur'an are to protect individuals from illegal sexual relations.

Marriage with believing maid:

'If any of you cannot afford to marry a free believing woman let him marry one of his believing maids whom he possesses. God best knows your faith. You are one of another. So marry them with their owner's permission, and give them their dower according to what is fair, neither committing fornication nor taking secret paramours.' (Qur'an:4:25)

During the time of Prophet (pbuh) slavery system was legal. Although Islam never approved of it but it followed a strategy by which the slavery system was gradually abolished. In the verse mentioned above there is command, if one cannot afford to marry a free believing woman, he can marry a believing maid with the permission of her master. It is also clarified that they are equal before God and they should not commit fornication.

- **Monasticism is not prescribed by God:**

Monasticism or monkhood is a religious way of life in which one renounces worldly life to devote oneself fully to spiritual work. The Almighty God sent many messengers from Prophet Adam to Prophet Mohammad for humanity's guidance, but none followed monasticism. All of them lived in a society like ordinary men; they conveyed the message of God to the people and put in their best efforts to reform people as per the guidance of the Almighty Lord.

"Then we sent after them our messengers, and we sent Jesus the son of Mary. We gave him the Gospel and imbued the hearts of those who followed him, with compassion and mercy. But we did not prescribe monasticism for them; that was their own innovation by which they sought to please God. But, they did not observe it in the way it should have been observed. So, we rewarded only those truly faithful, many of whom were disobedient." (Qur'an 57:26- 27)

In the above-quoted verse, God clarified that monasticism, practiced by some people in the name of religion, was the people's innovation. Neither God had ever prescribed it, nor had His messengers ever followed it. The life of Prophet Muhammad (pbuh) is the best role model for us. He neither practiced monasticism nor prescribed it to his followers.

From the verses quoted above it is clear, Islam promotes marriages in the society, it does not approve of monasticism and prescribes deterrent punishments for illegal sexual relations.

==================================

CHAPTER TEN

10. Qur'an and Marriages

"Today all good things have been made lawful to you. The food of the people of the Book (Jews and Christians) is lawful to you, and your food is lawful to them. The chaste believing women and the chaste women of those who were given the book before you, are lawful to you, provided you give them their dower (Maher) and marry them. Neither you should commit fornication nor keep them as a mistress."

(Qur'an 5:5)

All over the world, human societies are pluralistic, comprising people from various religions, races, languages and cultures living together, but marriages are primarily within the same faith. The reason is that people from the same religion have more or less the same way of life, traditions, festivals and rituals. In the verse mentioned above, the Omnipotent and Omniscient God has laid down specific rules for the Muslim community, which is as under.

First, all good things have been permitted by Almighty God for Muslims. Therefore they should not have any reservations and confusion about any good and useful thing available in society. We see many people around us are reluctant to eat and drink some items of food in the name of family tradition and religion.

Secondly, Muslims are permitted to consume the food items from the people of the Book. They are also allowed to eat the animals slaughtered by Jews and Christians. But, they are prohibited from consuming the animals slaughtered by members of other communities because they do not slaughter the animal in the name of Almighty God, Who created them for their consumption.

Thirdly, Muslims are permitted to marry unmarried women from the Jews and Christian communities. In the Qur'an actual word is 'Mohsinat,' which includes unmarried girls, divorced women and widows.

Christians and Jews both believe in the Almighty God, the Day of Judgment, the revelation of God in the form of the Gospel and the Torah, and they believe in all the messengers appointed by God from time to time, right from the first messenger of God, Prophet Adam. There is much similarity among them as far as items of faith and traditions are concerned. Probably this is the reason for the permission of marriage with them.

Another reason could be that Christians and Jews constitute a relatively large portion of the human population worldwide. Opening the door of marriage and sharing food would help bring them close to each other and give them a chance to understand Islam's teachings, which is the final version of divine guidance. This divine instruction helped spread Islam in West Asia, Africa and Europe during the medieval period of history, where a sizable population was either Christian or Jews. But due to the conservative attitude of masses such inter faith marriages are very rare in our society..

The above verse clarifies that Christian or Jew women are also entitled to the dower (Maher), as Muslim women are allowed. Also, Muslims are warned against illicit relations with anyone. Neither should they indulge in adultery nor have someone as mistress without formal marriage. In Islam, sexual relations are fully regulated and no illegal links are permitted, even with people of other religions. Probably due to this reason and Quranic guidance Muslims all over the world are able to protect their family system from disintegration.

- **Forbidden Matrimonial Relations**

"You are forbidden to take as wives your mothers, daughters, sisters, paternal and maternal aunts, your brother's daughters, your sister's daughters, your foster mothers, and foster sisters, your wives' mothers, and stepdaughters in your protection and the daughter of your wives with whom you have consummated your marriage, but if you have not consummated your marriage, then you will not be blamed (if you marry their daughters). You are also forbidden to marry spouses of your real sons or two sisters together, except for what has already passed. Indeed, God is All-Forgiving and Merciful. Also prohibited are married women, except those who have passed into your hands as prisoners of war. This is a commandment of God, and it is binding upon you. All women other than these are lawful to you, provided you seek them with your wealth, in honest wedlock, not in fornication. " (Qur'an 4:23-24)

Human society is the most complex society in the animal kingdom. It comprises a large number of family relations. It is practically impossible for a man to design law for human society that would consider various physical, biological, emotional, and psychological factors and do justice to it. Also there were many despicable practices regarding marriage in the world during the time of Prophet Muhammad. Therefore the Omniscient and All-Knowing God has provided detailed guidelines on this subject.

In the two verses mentioned above there is a list of all prohibited matrimonial relations. The list is exhaustive and can be categorized as under.

1. Blood relations: This includes mother, daughters, real sisters, paternal and maternal aunts, brother's daughters and sister's daughters.

2. Foster relations: This includes foster mother and foster sister. Foster mother means that has suckled a child of another woman or brings up her child as mother. Foster mother is as good as real mother for matrimonial purpose. Similarly, foster sister means daughter of his foster mother. She will be as good as his real sister for matrimonial purpose and they cannot marry with each other.

3. Blood relatives of wife: This includes mother in law and sisters in law.

4. Step daughter: It means the daughter of your wife from earlier marriage. Although there is no blood relationship between them but such marriage is prohibited.

5. Daughter of the wife with whom you have not consummated. There may be a case where although marriage is solemnized but husband and wife have never cohabited. In this case you are permitted to marry with her daughter after you divorce her mother.

6. Wife of real son:

7. Marriage with two real sisters: Two real sisters cannot be wives of a man simultaneously. However if one expires or is divorced then marriage can be solemnized.

8. Earlier mistakes and irregularities: All Forgiving and Merciful God has forgiven earlier irregularities. Laws are always designed for future and we find this strategy at many places in Qur'an.

9. Marriage with a married woman: No marriage can be solemnized with a woman who is already married. There is only one exception that is if she is a prisoner of war.

10. Adultery and fornication: Sexual relations are fully regulated in Islam and God has prescribed severe punishments for those who violate the divine commands, not only in this world but also in the Hereafter.

- **Marriage with father's wife:**

" Do not marry women whom your fathers married, except for what has already taken place in the past. This is indeed a shameful deed, a loathsome thing and an evil practice." (Qur'an: 4:22)

This was also one of the loathsome practices prevalent in some tribes where one would marry ones step mother after the death of father. God has prohibited it and called it a shameful, loathsome and evil practice.

- **Marriage with Polytheist**

"Do not marry mushrik women (who associate partners with God) until they become believers. A believer underprivileged woman is better than a woman who associates partners with God; however pleasing she may appear to you. (Likewise) do not wed your believing women to men who associate partners with God till they are believers. A believing underprivileged man is certainly better than a man who associates partners with God, even

though he may appear pleasing to you. Such people call you towards Hell and God calls you towards Paradise and forgiveness. He makes the message clear to people so that they may understand." (Qur'an 2 : 221)

The selection of a suitable match is a big problem in our society. The verse mentioned above, provides guidance to the believers on what should be their priority when considering their marriage partners. Association with God is an unpardonable sin, therefore when the foundation of a family is laid, we need to give utmost importance to this criterion and if we overlook this, there is every possibility of corruption of their faith and future generations' faith.

The purity of faith is so vital that God rated it above family wealth, beauty, and social status. In the above verse, God has declared that a believing underprivileged man is better for marriage than a polytheist man, even if they like him. And a believing underprivileged woman is better for marriage than a polytheist woman even if they like her.

- **Polygamy in Islam**

Give orphans their property, and do not exchange the bad for the good, and do not eat up their property by mixing it with your own. This, indeed, is a great sin.

And if you fear that you might not treat the orphan justly, then marry the women (their mothers) that seem good to you; two or three or four; but if you fear that you might not be able to treat them justly, then marry only one, or marry from among those whom you rightfully possess. This will make it more likely that you will avoid injustice. (Qur'an 4: 2-3)

In the above-quoted verse of the Quran, there is a solution to the problem of orphans and widows, which came up after the battle of Uhad between the Muslims and the Maccan army in which about seventy Muslims were martyred. The rehabilitation of their wives and children was a big problem for the small community of Muslims in Medina. At that time, the above verse was revealed by Prophet Muhammad, narrating how to solve the problem. As a result, several companions of the Prophet supported such families. Even Prophet himself married two such war widows. It's pertinent here to mention that out of the eleven wives of the Prophet, ten were either widow or divorced, and only Hazrat Ayesha was a bachelor at the time of marriage.

As the guidance of the Qur'an is for all times, we can draw general guidelines from the above verses of Qur'an.

1. Orphan's property:

In the above quoted verse God has given clear direction that orphan's property should be handed over to them, neither should it be exchanged with lesser valued property nor should it be consumed mixing it with your own property. This is considered as a great sin.

2. Taking care of orphans:

Muslims are asked to take due care of the orphans either supporting them from outside or they can include them as a family member by marrying their mothers. But it should be seen that no injustice is done to them.

3. Polygamy is conditional:

Looking at the background of these verses it can be inferred that the permission is conditional and not general. Here Muslims were asked to marry such widows may be two three or four in number depending upon their capacities to support such families. The limit of a maximum of four wives is drawn from this verse.

4. Justice to all wives:

There are explicit instructions for husbands to do justice if they have more than one wife. And if they can't do justice to them, then should marry only one wife. In this way, they will be able to avoid committing injustice which is punishable in the court of Almighty God.

Thus verses mentioned above provide a solution to the problem of orphans and widows. Polygamy is not permitted in general as a means of pleasure and entertainment for Muslim men, as contended by some people. When we study the life history of Prophet Muhammad (pbuh) we find that his first marriage was with a widow Khadija (R,A.) who was forty while he was only twenty five. He lived with her for twenty four years and had six children from her, but never thought of second marriage. After the death of Khadija he married with Saoda (R.A.) who was also a widow and aged around fifty five. Thus we can infer that polygamy is not a general rule but it is allowed in some conditions,

===================================

CHAPTER ELEVEN

11. Role of Spouses under Islam

Although the institution of family is universal, there is no universal law in human society to clarify the role of husband and wife in the family. As a result many marriages fail and families break apart. In our community, we follow various norms, practices, and traditions but they are inadequate to solve various marital issues and family disputes. Almighty God, the Creator of humanity, has provided excellent guidance in Qur'an. We would like to study a few verses on the topic.

"***Husbands are protectors of wives because God has blessed some of them over others and because they spend their wealth on them. And virtuous women are obedient and guard the rights of husbands in their absence, which God has protected.......*" (Qur'an 4:34)**

This verse covers following points.

- **Husband protects wife:**

In Quran, the word used for the protector is 'Qawwam,' a broad term covering the meaning of protector, caretaker, controller, leader, or in charge. In common parlance, we may call it head or boss. There is no denying the fact that

God has blessed man with more physical strength and qualities like bravery, self confidence and decision making capacity. Probably due to these qualities husbands are given the responsibility of protection of the family. The wordings of the above-quoted verse are descriptive and not in the form of command or order. This shows there is flexibility in drawing lessons. Keeping in view these points we should design our family life.

- **The husband provides finance for the family**:

The husband is responsible for all the financial needs of the family. All over the world we find, right from tribal societies to modern urban societies; generally, men perform the duties of earning, and women concentrate on home or home-based activities. God has nowhere stopped women from engaging themselves in economic, social, or other activities.

- **A virtuous wife is obedient to her husband**:

Once it is settled that the husband is the boss of the homely affairs, as a part of discipline wife should obey her husband in all reasonable matters. This does not mean that a man should not consult his wife or others in the family before taking any important decision. Mutual consultations are always good and create positive family environment. And once the decision is taken others should obey. In this way we can develop a happy family.

- **A virtuous wife takes due care of house:**

Another quality of a virtuous wife is, she takes due care of the house in the absence of her husband including children and other family members, guests, properties, etc. If a woman can develop these two qualities in her, she would be able to make a happy home.

- Spouses are like the garment to each other:

"They are like a garment to you, and you are like a garment to them."(Qur'an 2:187)

In this verse, the Almighty God has used a beautiful simile to describe the role of husband and wife in a family. We know that garments serve three needs. i) To cover private parts, ii) to protect the body from dust, sun, and severe weather, and iii) to make us good-looking and graceful. If both husband and wife take due care of each other's needs, likes and dislikes, they will be to make a good and happy family.

- Husband is like a farmer:

'Your wives are a place of sowing of seed for you, so go into your place of cultivation as you wish. And do good for yourselves, and fear God, and know that you shall meet Him. And give good tidings to those who believe. (Qur'an 2:223)

In verse mentioned above, Omniscient God has metaphorically called the wives a place of sowing seed or farm. If we closely observe the life of a farmer, we find that he is a sincere, hardworking and thoughtful man. He plans his work well in advance, prepares his farm well before sowing, waters it on time, and is watchful of its crop when it grows. Likewise, a husband is expected to take care of his wife. He should work hard to earn a livelihood for his wife and children and care for their health, education, and welfare. He should also pray to God for their success and should always remain conscious of Him before he will be presented on the Day of Judgment.

- Behave decently with wife

Believers, it is not lawful for you to become heirs or guardians of women against their will, nor should you apply undue pressure so that you may take away a part of what you have given them unless they are guilty of brazenly immoral conduct. Live with them decently; if you dislike them, it may be that you dislike something in which God has placed much good for you. (Qur'an 4:19)

The verse mentioned above contains following points.

- The verse mentioned above clearly prohibits a husband from using his wife's property without her consent. If she happily allows it, there is no problem. Otherwise, her property should not be used even for domestic expenditure.
- Whatever a husband has given to his wife in the form of a dower (Maher) or gifts, he should not take them back in case of divorce. The only exception is when a woman is guilty of explicit immoral conduct.

- Husbands should treat their wives decently; they should neither put undue pressure nor subject them to abuse and violence. Hot arguments, foul language and violence should be avoided.
- Lastly, Almighty God has advised the husband to ignore minor shortcomings he finds in his wife because no

individual is free from faults. Moreover, he does not know what virtues are hidden in his wife's conduct.

- God has created love between spouses :

"Another of His signs is that He has created for you spouses from among yourselves, so that you may find peace in them, and He has created between you affection and kindness. Truly, there are signs in this for the people who reflect." (Qur'an 30 :21)

In the above verse, Allah God has mentioned four points which are discussed as under.

- **God makes spouses:**

'He has created for you your spouse.' It means it is the God who decides the spouses. In fact only God decides in which family and place a child should be born. No one has power to select his family or place of birth. Similarly, nobody knows who will be his or her spouse in future and who will be their children.

- **Marriage for mutual peace:**

. After the marriage both the partners should make conscious efforts to lead a happy and peaceful life. They should know that their marriage was decided by God and so they should try their best to make it successful. There may be some problems but they should try to solve them in the best possible way.

- **Affection and kindness between spouses:**

God has created the emotions of love and kindness between the spouses. It is this emotional bond of love and kindness that binds husband and wife together for life. It is this bond which ultimately proves to be the strongest of all social bonds. This is the blessing of God and we should be thankful to Him for His benevolence.

- **Signs of God:**

The above mentioned verse starts with the words, "Another of His sign is that", and then He describes His three blessings: selection of spouses, marriage for mutual peace, affection and kindness between spouses. God says these are His signs that mean if people think over these blessings they will surely understand His greatness.

- **Protect your marriage:**

We should remember that spouses are selected by God, so once there is marriage, we should try to preserve this relationship as far as possible. This is exemplified in the parables ofProphet Noah and Prophet Lot.

"***Allah has set forth for the unbelievers the parable of the wives of Noah and Lot. They were wedded to two of our righteous servants (Prophet Noah and Prophet Lot), but each disobeyed her husband. Their husbands could be of no avail to them before God. They were told to enter the Fire along with all the others who would enter it." (Qur'an - 66: 10)***

Prophet Noah continued to live with his disobedient wife till the advent of divine punishment in the form of the Great Deluge. Similarly, Prophet Lot continued his conjugal life till the last night, when Allah asked him to leave her behind for divine punishment. Both these stories tell us that family life should not be disturbed even if there is dispute in faith.

- **Save your family from the Hell:**

"O, Believers! Safe guard yourselves and your families from the Fire whose fuel is human beings and stones and which is watched over by stern and powerful angels who never disobey God's commands and promptly do as they are commanded. (Qur'an 66:6)

In the above-quoted verse of the Quran, all believers are commanded to safeguard themselves and their family members from Hell. Therefore parents should see that children get both religious and modern education, they do not acquire bad habits from the society, they are regular in prayer, and they read good books and magazines. Parents should spend their quality time with the children so that they are well aware of their progress and development. In addition to parents if there are other adult members in the family they should also take care of children.

In the holy Quran, we find the prayers of the Messengers of God in some places. They tell us how we should pray.

- **Prayer of Prophet Abraham for family:**

"My Lord! Make me steadfast in prayer, and so also my children. My Lord, do accept my invocation. My Lord! Forgive me and my parents and the believers on the day of accounting (Day of Judgment)

(Qur'an 14:40-41)

The above verses show that Prophet Abraham prayed for himself, his children, his parents, and all the believers. Therefore we should also pray to God for our family members and include this prayer in our daily supplications.

- **Prayer of Prophet Zachariah**

There is another prayer from Prophet Zachariah.

"Then Zachariah prayed to his Lord, saying, O Lord, grant me by your grace a virtuous child. You alone hear all the prayers." (Qur'an 3:38)

Prophet Zachariah was the patron of Mary, the mother of Jesus Christ. When he learned that God had arranged unseasonal fruit for Mary, he also prayed to the Almighty God for a virtuous child. Allah accepted his prayer and blessed him with a son in old age. His name was Yahiya (pbuh). Some parents don't have children because of which they remain under stress. From the life history of Prophet Zachariah we learn that God blessed him with a son at a very old age when there was hardly any possibility of child. So we should always be positive and continue our prayer supplications.

From the above-quoted verses of the Quran, we learn, it is our responsibility to take due care of our children and other family members. We should do our best to make them good and virtuous persons to save them from the Fire of Hell. Secondly, we should include our parents, our children and all the believers in our invocations and prayers.

- **Divine Advice to the wives of the Prophet**

"O wives of the Prophet! You are not like other women. If you fear God, do not be too soft-spoken in your speech, lest anyone whose heart is deceased should be tempted. But do speak decently. And stay peacefully in your homes and do not flaunt your charms as in the former times of ignorance. Establish prayers and pay Zakat and obey God and His messenger. God only wishes to remove all impurities from you and purify you completely." (Qur'an 33: 32-33)

Although the two verses mentioned above are mainly addressed to the wives of Prophet Mohammad (pbuh), they apply to all respectable women in general. We know that Prophet Mohammad was not only a religious head but also a judicial, administrative, and political authority. As such, many people used to come to him for various purposes. He and his family did not live in a fort or castle but in tiny houses near Masjide Nabvi in Medina. So, there was a risk to the safety and security of the wives of the Prophet (pbuh). This was the background over which the above verses of the Qur'an were revealed that cover following points

There are five commands of Allah to the wives of the Prophet

- While talking to unknown men, they should take due precautions. They should neither be too soft and courteous nor too harsh and rude but should be decent and formal. This is to avoid the chances of misunderstanding and undue temptations.
- They should concentrate on homes and domestic affairs and whenever they are required to move out, they should take due precautions. They should avoid displaying their charms and beauty to the general public.

- Like men, they are also bound to perform regular prayers and pay Zakat for their wealth.
- They should also obey God and His messenger. Just because they are wives of the prophet they do not have any privilege or remission from various obligations and duties.
- If they follow the above guidelines, God will cleanse them from evils and make them pure.

All the above commands to the wives of the Prophet are also applicable to the general women. Similarly there are other verses of the Qur'an, although they are directly addressed to Prophet Mohammad but they are applicable to all.

- **Advice your children:**

Home is the first school of a child. It is here that he learns important lessons of his life and how to live in society. Experts of personality development say seventy-five percent of a child's personality develops in the first six years. Parents are the best role model for their children. So they should try to present ideal role models for their children. They should closely watch their children and offer them suitable advice so that they become good human.

"Luqman said to his son while counseling him, "My son, do not associate anything with God. Surely associating others with Him is a terrible sin." (Qur'an 31:13)

"(He further said) O' my son though your deed is as small as a mustard seed, and though it be hidden inside a rock, or in the heavens, or on the earth, God will bring it forth. Truly, God is fully aware of even the smallest things.

O' my dear son! Say your prayers regularly, enjoin virtues,forbid evils, and endure patiently whatever affliction may befall you. Surely these are great deeds.

And don't show your arrogance to people, and do not walk with pride upon the earth; for God does not like arrogant and boastful people. Walk modestly and keep your voice low (while talking); for the ugliest of all voices is the braying of the ass." ((Qur'an 31:16-19)

The above quoted verses of Qur'an are the advice of Luqman (pbuh) to his son which cover following points..

- Do not associate anything with God. It is a terrible sin. This means he should not worship any other deity except God. He should not treat anyone equal to God or make him Allah's partner.
- All your deeds big or small, hidden or explicit are known to God and He will present them before you on the Day of Judgment. Therefore you should be cautious.
- Be regular in prayers. Regularity in prayer is a must for us. There are some who pray but are not regular. Regular prayer makes a person self disciplined.
- Enjoin virtues and forbid evils. It means it is not sufficient to do good deeds but one should advice others to do good work. Secondly, if we have capacity we should stop others from doing evils.
- Be patient in difficult situation. Life is never smooth sailing all the way. There are ups and downs in life. Parents should guide their children to show patience and forbearance in facing difficulties by quoting various examples. Being patient in difficulties is a great quality.
- Don't be arrogant. Arrogance and boasting are two negative qualities that spoil the personality of individuals. We should see that they do not develop in

our children. Arrogance is the main quality of Iblis the Satan, who was condemned by God for his arrogance. Satan is also called Alghuroor for this reason.

- Don't walk with pride. One should avoid walking on the road proudly to impress others, instead he should walk modestly.
- Talk softly. The way we talk reflects our personality. So when we talk, we should keep our voice low without showing our pride. God has compared high pitch voice with the braying of the donkey.

The above verses of the Qur'an provide very comprehensive guidance to both husbands and wives about their role and responsibilities in the development of their families. If we can follow them in true spirit we will be able to build successful family.

============================ ========

CHAPTER TWELVE

12. Procedure of Divorce

People marry to live a happy family life, have children and maintain lifelong matrimonial relationship. But there are some who fail to maintain this bond of marriage for long and decide to divorce this relation due to various reasons. While studying Quran we find there are verses to guide us whom we can marry and whom we cannot, but there is no description as how to perform marriage. On the other hand we find there are many verses that deal with divorce and if we arrange them in proper order we get a complete procedure of divorce. We learn from these verses that divorce is not any impulsive and instant action to dissolve a marriage as some people think but it is a well thought of action plan and procedure that has to be witnessed properly. Also, there is a Hadees from Prophet (pbuh) that out of all the lawful things God dislikes divorce the most. So we should be cautious about the right of divorce. We would like to study this problem in the light of verses of the Qur'an.

"***And for the women, you fear rebellion, admonish them, remain apart in beds, and tell them (the consequences of***

disobedience). If they obey you, then do not seek ways to harm them. Allah is Exalted and Great." (Qur'an 4:34)

- **Valid reason for divorce:**

The option of divorce should not be exercised on flimsy ground or minor misconduct but it can be exercised when there is major problem of disobedience and misconduct. In such a situation husbands are advised not to take any spontaneous action in anger about divorce but instead should follow a well thought of action plan.

- First Step: The husband should admonish her verbally about the mistake or misbehavior and give her some time for correction; if she obeys and corrects herself then the matter should end.

- Second Step: In case there is no improvement then he should stop sharing bedroom with her and again give her some time for improvement. If there is an improvement, the matter should be closed.
- Third Step: If the defiance continues then he should clearly warn her of the consequences. Again he should give some time, and if there is improvement then she should not be harmed. But if there is no improvement next step can be taken.

- **Appointment of Arbiters:**

"If you fear any breach or discord between a husband and his wife, appoint one arbiter from his family and one from her family. If they both want to set the things right, God will bring reconciliation between them. He is all-

knowing and all aware." (Qur'an 4:35)

The verse mentioned above is about the appointment of arbiters. When we fear there is likelihood of separation we should appoint arbiters to resolve the problem. One arbiter should be appointed from the husband's side and one from the wife's side. Family members and friends familiar with the issues can be appointed arbiters. They should try their best to resolve the issue and save the marriage. But if the problem is not solved through arbitrage, the next step of divorce can be undertaken as described below.

- **Procedure of divorce:**

Once it is decided by the parties to dissolve the marriage they should approach Islamic court or family court. Qazi or judge will also try to reconcile the parties to his satisfaction and may give some more time for reconciliation. If this attempt of reconciliation also fails the Qazi or Judge will prepare a divorce document. It will contain all the conditions of divorce like, waiting period or Iddat, maintenance during the waiting period, residential accommodation, custody of small children if any, details of assets and liabilities, etc. This event must also be witnessed by at least two respectable persons. Documents must be duly signed. A copy of the document may be given to both the parties.

- **Requirement of two witnesses:**

And when their waiting term is ended, either keep them honorably or part with them in honors. Call to witness two reliable men from among you, and bear faithful witness of God. This is advice for those who believe in God and the

last day. Allah will find a way out for him who fears Allah. (Qur'an 65:2)

The verse mentioned above tells us

- When the waiting period is about to reach, they will have to decide whether to live together or to separate. Two witnesses should be called, and formalities should be completed properly to avoid misunderstandings and confusion. If they choose to reconcile, there is no need for remarriage, but the divorce will be final if the waiting period ends.

- The woman's dignity and honor must be protected during this divorce process. This is advice from a knowing God. After divorce and completion of the waiting period, a woman can marry any other person of her choice.

- **Waiting period for divorce**

"But if they decide upon divorce, God is all Hearing and All-Knowing. Divorced women should wait for three menstrual cycles. It is unlawful for them to hide what God has created in their wombs if they believe in God and the last day. Their husbands have the right to take them back within that time if they desire to be reconciled. And the wives have rights corresponding to those the husbands have, according to what is considered fair. But the husbands have a rank above them. God is All-powerful, All-wise." (Qur'an 2:227-228)

The verse mentioned above covers the following points

- The Iddat or waiting period starts from the date of divorce and ends at the expiry of three menstrual cycles. Islamic jurists opine, if the erstwhile couple decides to revert during the period of Iddat, no Nikah formalities are necessary; they can express their intention to revoke the divorce. However, after the period of Iddat, all formalities of Nikah will have to be performed if they want to live together.
- The woman should not hide her pregnancy. And if she is pregnant at the time of divorce, the term of Iddat will extend up to the delivery of the child.
- For the reconciliation husband and wife both can take the initiative. Parties can also engage the services of counselors to resolve the problem. As far as divorce is concerned, men are given the upper hand. He can decide to divorce; however, the wife cannot make such a unilateral decision. For divorce, she will have to follow the procedure of Khula.

- **Additional guidelines for the waiting period:**

"In case of those of your wives who have passed the age of menstruation, if you have any doubt, know that their waiting period is three months, and that will apply likewise to those who have not yet menstruated; the waiting period of those who are pregnant will be until they deliver, their burden (baby). God makes things easy for those who are mindful of Him. Such is the commandment that God has revealed to you. He, who fears God, his sins shall be forgiven, and he shall be richly rewarded." (Qur'an 65:4-5)

The above-quoted two verses have guidelines for all exceptional situations. The waiting period is fixed as three months for pre-menstruation conditions, menu pauses, or any other medical problem. It also covers the case when there is doubt about menstruation. If the woman is pregnant, the waiting period will extend until her delivery. After that, the divorce is finalized, and the woman cannot live with her ex-husband. While following the procedure of divorce it should always be remembered that God the sublime is watching them and they are accountable to Him on the Day of Judgment.

- **Do not expel the wife from the house during the waiting period:**

"O Prophet! When you divorce wives, divorce them for their waiting- period (Iddat), and count the waiting period accurately; and be conscious of God your Lord. Do not drive them out of their homes (during the waiting period), nor should they leave unless they are guilty of explicit immoral conduct. These are the limits set by God. One who transgresses God's limits does wrong to one's self. You never know. After that, God may well bring about some new situation." (Qur'an 65:1)

The verse mentioned above conveys the following points.

The wife should not be asked to vacate the house soon after the divorce, nor should she leave the house herself during the waiting period. There is every possibility that parties may realize their mistakes and turn towards reconciliation. If they revert during the Iddat period, there is no need for Nikah and they can continue their conjugal life, but they should declare their intention to revoke the divorce. This event should also be witnessed by two reliable persons and recorded.

Secondly, the wife can be asked to leave the house if there is a case of gross moral misconduct. However, both parties are warned by the Almighty God not to trespass the limits. He is witness to all their doings.

Unfortunately, some do not follow this procedure and make instant divorce decisions by pronouncing the word Talaq and sending the wife to her parents or relatives. Thus they not only disobey divine commands but also create many problems for the families.

- **The Separation without Divorce:**

"For those who swear that they will not approach their wives, there shall be a waiting period of four months. If they revert to conciliation, surely God is most forgiving and merciful." (Qur'an 2:226)

Sometimes, people swear not to approach their wives but do not openly declare divorce. This is not permitted by God. There is clear instruction in the above verse that they must decide within four months whether they want to continue the marriage or divorce. They cannot keep the marriage doubtful for more than four months.

Today thousands of cases regarding marital problems and divorce are pending in various courts because of which both the parties suffer, not only they waste precious time and money but also peace of mind. In fact matrimonial disputes should be resolved as early as possible in the interest of society. We can take clue from the Qur'an and fix four month's period as a limit for deciding any matrimonial dispute.

==================================

CHAPTER THIRTEEN

13. Post Divorce issues

This chapters covers some of the issues related to divorce that are not covered in the divorce chapter, they are dealt with in this chapter.

- **Divorce When Marriage is not consummated**

There may be instances when the couple does not get a chance to come together after marriage. It may be due to far-off distance, family dispute, medical problems, child marriage, etc. In such cases, there is no need to observe the Iddat or waiting period. However, even here, as a noble gesture, God has advised husbands to pay something to the women even though no physical contact is made. The reference verse of Quran is as under.

Believers! If you marry believing women and divorce them before the marriage is consummated, you are not required to count the waiting period. But do make provisions for them and release them honorably. (Qur'an 33:49)

There is no denying the fact that whenever a marriage breaks, there is some damage to the self-respect and reputation of the parties, especially the women. All-knowing God has taken into account this aspect and has advised the man to show benevolence and present some gift to the divorced woman.

- **When Maher is fixed but marriage is not consummated**

If you divorce them before the marriage is consummated but after their dower has been settled, give them half of their dower money unless they agree to forego it, or the man in whose hand lies the knot of marriage forgives it (Parent or guardian). To forego is near to righteousness. Do not miss any chance of benevolence towards each other. God is witness to whatever you do." (Qur'an 2:237)

In the earlier verse, the quantum of compensation was not mentioned. Here it is clarified as half of the dower amount. But in this verse, there is advice for the bride and her guardians. If they forego their right, it is better. God has rated such people as righteous and conscientious. By offering compensation, the groom or groom side may feel elated, and by refusing such compensation, the bride and the bride side may feel pleased. Thus it is a win-win situation and both are satisfied.

Lastly, there is general advice for all to show benevolence and generosity in dealings. This is a panacea for many psychological and emotional ailments. We can solve many problems by being kinder, more generous, and forgiving.

- **Maintenance of Women during Iddat**

"Let the woman (who are undergoing waiting period) live in the same place and in accordance to your means; and

do not harass them in order to make their lives difficult. If they are pregnant, maintain them until they give birth; if they suckle your infants, pay them for it; discuss things among yourselves, in all decency. Let another woman suckle for you if you cannot bear with each other. Let the man of means spend in accordance with his means; and let him whose resources are limited spend by what God has given him. God does not burden any person with more than He has given him. God will soon bring about ease after hardship. (Qur'an 65:6-7)

After divorce, maintenance of woman specially non-earning woman is the biggest problem that we face. Almighty God has duly addressed this problem and provided detailed guidance in the Qur'an.

First, the woman is asked to remain in the same house and need not immediately vacate the house and go to her parents or other relatives. The idea is to provide a chance for the parties to rethink their divorce in the changed situation. This strategy may enable parties to reconcile. Secondly, the husband is advised to make full lodging boarding and other arrangements for the divorcee as per his standard of living. In this way the problem of maintenance of the divorcee during the intervening period is also solved. Thirdly, a woman should not be harassed or compelled to leave the house during this period. This is against the divine guidelines, and the husband will be liable for punishment in the court of Almighty God. Fourthly, the maintenance period in the case of pregnancy is until the delivery of the child. Fifthly, the choice is given to the parties about nursing after delivery. If they agree that the mother should suckle the baby, then man should provide adequate maintenance to the mother. In this situation, parties are free to make their own decisions. There is no command from God. As a rule, He does not burden any person more than his capacity. Lastly, God has asked both parties to show forbearance. Hard times never last long. God is extremely merciful. Soon He would bless them with good times.

- **Husbands should not take back their Gifts**

"If you desire to replace one wife with another, do not take back any part of the property from her, even if you have given her a treasure. Would you take it back by leveling false charges against her and committing an explicit sin." (Qur'an 4:20)

After the divorce possession of property is a major cause of dispute. Almighty God has addressed this problem too in His Book and provided a perfect solution. Husbands are advised not to take back what they have given them as a gift during their married life even if it is a treasure. Despite this explicit order, if someone disobeys God, he should be prepared for punishment from his Lord. Secondly, any effort to get back the property from an unwilling ex-wife would generate more enmity and hatred. As a result, they would not be able to lead peaceful life even after divorce. Similarly, all doors of future reconciliation would be closed forever. Therefore, men should refrain from it. Thirdly, Husband should not try to level false charges of immoral conduct against her to get back the property given away as a gift. This is a great sin before God. There is a provision in Qur'an, if the wife is guilty of immoral conduct then husband can take back the gifts that he had given to his wife. (Qur'an: 4: 19). But this provision should not be misused otherwise there is warning from God.

Fourthly, this provision of not to take back gifts acts as a deterrent to a person for exercising divorce specially when he had given her some property as a gift. Thus we can say that Almighty God has provided a wonderful solution to believers to resolve the issue of divorce.

- **Provision for Divorcee:**

"For divorced women, a provision according to what is fair shall also be made. This is an obligation binding on the righteous. Thus God makes His commandments clear to you so that you may understand. (Quran2:241)

Like maintenance in the case of widows, there is the provision of maintenance for divorced women too; however, in this case, the period is not specified and it is left to be decided by both the parties by mutual consultation or by the court, keeping in view the causes of divorce and financial conditions of the parties concerned.

Divorce should not result in hostility; it should only be considered an undesirable eventuality where both partners agree to break the marriage bond and decide to lead their lives independently. Hence, husbands who are often financially stronger than their wives are asked to make a fair provision for them.

Often it is seen that after divorce, both parties take extreme positions. The man does not want to give anything and levels false allegations; the woman and her blood relatives want to extract a maximum portion of her ex-husband's earnings. As a result, the acrimony increases and litigations in the court of law begin, which continues for years. Thus even after divorce, both parties live an unhappy life.

=====================================

CHAPTER FOURTEEN

14. Remarriage after divorce

"When you divorce woman, and they reach the end of their waiting period, do not prevent them from marrying other men, if they mutually agree as per norms. This is an advice to one who believes in God and the last Day. This is more virtuous and purer for you. God knows (better), and you do not know." (Qur'an 2:232)

In the verse quoted above there are instructions about the remarriage of the divorcee. A divorced woman is free to marry any man of her choice once she completes iddat. Ex-husband or his family members should not come in the way of her second marriage. It is not only immoral but not liked by God. Hence there is clear instruction not to prevent her second marriage. It should be remembered that during Iddat or the waiting period, husband and wife can revert and unite without marriage therefore all the formalities of remarriage should be undertaken only after the end of Iddat period. In some families, women are not allowed to remarry after the divorce or death of their husbands in the name of family prestige and dignity. But we should know as per Quranic teachings there is no such restriction.

- **Only two Divorces are Revocable:**

Divorce may be exercised twice; thereafter a woman may be retained honorably or released with kindness. And it is not lawful for you to take back anything of what you have given your wives, unless both fear that they would not be able to observe the bounds set by God. In such a case it shall be no sin for either of them, if the woman opts to give something. These are the bounds set by God; do not transgress them. Those who transgress the bounds of God are sinners. (Qur'an 2:229)

The verse mentioned above clarifies the following points

1) The option of remarriage after divorce is available only twice. A man can divorce his wife and reunite without marriage during the Iddat period and with a second Nikah after the Iddat period. Subsequently, if there is another divorce, he can again reunite with her wife during the Iddat period without Nikah and after the Iddat period with the third Nikah, subject to the consent of her wife. But after the third divorce, he cannot marry her ex-wife as remarriage after the third divorce is not permitted ordinarily.

2) After completing the formality of divorce and Iddat the woman should honourably be allowed to return to her home. It is better if she is given some gift as a noble gesture at the time of departure.

3) Whatever dowers, gifts, jewellery, cash, property, etc., were given to the wife should not be taken back. However, there may be an exceptional situation where the parties can't comply with the above guidelines. Here, the woman has a choice of returning certain items if it is required for an amicable separation.

Take the case of a man who had purchased a house out of his earnings in his wife's name and has no other home. Now for specific reasons, there is a divorce between them.

Legally wife is entitled to hold complete possession of her home and she can even ask her ex-husband to vacate the house but if the husband does not have a second house to shift to, there would be a major problem. In this situation the wife can allow partitioning the house or vacating the house for her husband and children as a good gesture; Allah has given these discretionary rights to the wife.

In the last portion of the verse there is a warning to the people not to transgress the boundaries set by God.

Provision ofMarriage after the third divorce:

"And if a man divorces his wife (for the third time), he cannot remarry her until she has married another man. Then, if the next husband divorces her, there will be no blame on either of them either of them if the former husband and wife return to one another, provided they think they can keep within the bounds set by God. These are the limits God prescribes, which He makes clear to the man of understanding. (Qur'an 2:230)

Although this may be a remote possibility, the Merciful God has made a provision in the Qur'an for such an eventuality. So when a man has exercised his right of divorce three times, he cannot remarry the ex-wife. However, there is an exception. If the woman marries another man and he too divorces her voluntarily for some reasons, there is a chance for the woman to remarry her first husband provided both agree to live peacefully thereafter.

====================================

CHAPTER FIFTEEN

15. Miscellaneous Family Issues

- **Maintenance for Widows:**

Provision of maintenance for widows and divorcees is a very sensitive and controversial problem in our community as there are diverse views on this subject. Here we would like to understand this problem in the light of Quranic verses.

"And those of you who die and leave widows, there is a bequest for them of an year's maintenance, and they should not be evicted from homes; but if they leave the place of their own, you may not be blamed for what they may likely choose to do for themselves. And God is Almighty and wise. (Qur'an 2:240)

The above verse should be seen in the context of a joint family system. If a man dies and he leaves behind him a widow as an heir, then members of the family are advised to provide maintenance for one year. Provision of maintenance after one year is discretionary.

Secondly, the widow should not be compelled to vacate the house where she resides. A year's period is normally sufficient for making an alternate arrangement. During this period, she can decide on her remarriage. If she is married, she can shift to her new husband, but if she is not married, she can negotiate with her in-laws and blood relatives about her stay. In such cases, arriving at a fair solution is often very difficult. Therefore Almighty God did not provide any clear-cut guidelines and left it to the common wisdom of the parties.

People must take a sympathetic view and solve the problem amicably without hurting anybody. After all, God is watching all of them. And He will take account of all that they do. In such cases, we should not forget the elements of benevolence and generosity. We find so many verses in Qur'an that ask for charity and expenditure in the way of God, so in such a situation we should take a very sympathetic view and see that the widow is properly settled.

Lastly, the widow is free to plan her future life, and the family members should respect her decision. If she wants to marry again after the Iddat no one should object. Although, in our present society there are some reluctance about remarriage of widows but there is need to create awareness about this issue. Permission of more than one marriage is actually kept in Islam to solve the problem of divorcees and widows. This is practically demonstrated by Prophet (pbuh). Out of eleven of his wives ten were either widows or divorcees.

- **Widow Remarriage:**

And those of you who die and leave widows, such widows should restrain themselves for four months and ten days. And when they have reached the end of their waiting period, you will not be blamed for what they may reasonably choose

to do with themselves. And God is aware of what you do. (Qur'an 2:234)

From the above-quoted verse, it is clear that in the case of the husband's death, the waiting period is four months and ten days. After this period the divorcee is free to decide about her marriage. In some communities, widow remarriage is considered highly objectionable even today, despite the permission of God and positive civil laws. There is a great need to educate the people in this regard. In this male dominated society, life of a single woman is full of problems and dangers, so there is need to develop awareness in the society.

- **Nursing of Baby after Divorce**

"And the (divorced) mothers should nurse their children for two whole years if they wish to complete the period of nursing. And during this period, the father of the child shall be responsible for the maintenance of the mother, in a reasonable manner. No person is burdened with more than he or she can bear. No mother shall be made to suffer on account of her child, and no father shall be made to suffer on account of his child. The same duties devolve upon the father's heir (in case of the father's death). But if, after mutual consultation, they agree to wean the child, there shall be no blame on them. Nor shall it be any objection if you desire to engage a wet nurse for your children, provided you pay what you have agreed to pay as per norm. Have a fear of God, and know that God is observant of all your actions." (Qur'an 2:233)

Divorce is an end of a social contract and not the beginning of a chapter of animosity. The child's interest should be protected even if the marriage breaks down. Its nursing problem should be settled amicably without hurting anyone. The terms of the contract should be clear and transparent.

If both parties agree, the mother should nurse the child until it reaches two years age. In that case, the father has to bear complete maintenance of the child and the mother. If there is no agreement on nursing between the two parties, another foster mother may nurse the baby. Both parties should take the decision, keeping in view that God is seeing them and they must face him in the Hereafter.

Unreasonable demands from the mother should not harass the child's father, nor should the child's mother be subjected to harassment by the father or his relatives, taking advantage of the other's weakness. But if the nursing is done by the foster mother, she must be fully paid as per the terms of the contract.

- **Taking Care of orphans**

In every society there are children who lose their parents one or both in young age, they are called orphans. To bring them up is the responsibility of the society and specially the relatives. There are some noble souls in the society who are willing to patronize them, treat them well and bring them up till they are adults. But there are some guardians who maltreat them, exploit them and try to usurp their property dishonestly. Therefore Almighty God revealed explicit guidelines and warned people to take due care of the orphans and do justice to them.

a. ***"Consumption of orphan's property is a great sin:***

And give to the orphans their properties; do not exchange good things with bad things, and do not consume their properties by mixing them with your own. Indeed, this is a great sin." (Qur'an 4:2)

In the above verse, there are explicit directions to the guardians to return their property to the orphans fully. Just because they are weak, their good property should neither be exchanged with bad property nor be usurped. There is a warning to them from their Lord.

a. **Take due care of orphans, as Almighty God is watching you:**

"Keep a close check on orphans till they attain the age of marriage. Then if you find them mature of mind, hand over their property to them. Do not consume it excessively and hastily before they are adults. If the guardian is affluent, let him abstain altogether, and if he is poor, let him have what is just and reasonable for himself. And when you hand over their property to them, call witnesses upon them; although God is sufficient to take account."

(Qur'an 4:6) In this verse, some additional instructions are given to the guardians. They should take due care of orphans till they reach the age of marriage or maturity and hand over their property to them. If guardians are poor, they are allowed to use a reasonable part of the property of the orphans for their nursing, but if they are affluent, they should desist from consuming their property. Lastly, they are asked to hand over the property to the orphans in the presence of witnesses, although Almighty God is sufficient to take into account.

====================================

CHAPTER SIXTEEN

16. Quran, Dress Code and Hijab

No living being except humans has the privilege of wearing clothes. So we may call it the unique feature of a human society. God has made it obligatory for mankind to wear proper attire and cover their nakedness. If they disobey His command, they are liable for punishment in the Hereafter. Hijab is a broad term that includes dress code for men and women, etiquettes of man and woman interactions, partition or separation of ladies and gents, etc. There are detailed guidelines in Qur'an both for men and women so we would like to study them in this chapter.

- **Purpose of clothes:**

O' children of Adam! We have blessed you with garments to cover your nakedness and have made it a thing of beauty, but the garment of God-consciousness (Taqwa) is the best. Here in lies a message from God so that people may learn from it. (Qur'an 7:26)

The verse mentioned above describes two main objectives of wearing clothes. i) To cover nakedness. For men it is obligatory to cover body from the naval to the knees when in public. This is called as 'Sater' of males. For women the 'Sater' inclides covering all parts of body except face hands and feet. They should take special care to cover these parts before opposite sex. To cover the remaining part of body is optional. ii) Properly stitched dress improves the looks and personality of a person, therefore one should try to put on good clothes if one can afford. Both these clothing objectives should be kept in mind when we purchase clothes. It is also clarified in the above verse that 'Taqwa' is the best garment. By 'Taqwa,' we mean character, morality, and fear of God. So we should take care of our clothes as well as our character.

- **Instructions to men about Hijab:**

"Tell believing men to control their gaze and remain chaste, this will be most conducive to their purity. Verily God is aware of all that they do. (Qur'an 24:30)

In the verse mentioned above there are two instructions for men as under.

Muslim men are asked to control their gaze, which means they should avoid looking at indecent and shameful things. They should take special care to control their gaze when they look at women. This is the first step in the direction of Hijab by which they can prevent vices from entering their mind.

They are asked to protect their private parts and chastity. This is the second step to follow Hijab guidelines. By covering their intimate body parts properly, they can avoid many undesirable vices. They are also asked to remain chaste, that means they should not indulge in any unlawful sexual relationship.

- **Instruction to women about Hijab:**

"And tell believing woman to control their gaze and remain chaste, and not to reveal their charms save what is normally apparent thereof; and they should fold their shawls or dupattas over their bosoms."

"They can reveal their charms and adornments only to their husbands, or their fathers, or their husbands fathers, or their sons or their husbands sons, or their brothers, or their brothers' sons, or their sisters' sons, or maid servants or their slaves and servants, or their male attendants who have no sexual desire, or children who still have no carnal knowledge of women. Nor should they walk indecently to draw attention to their hidden charms. And O believers, all of you should turn to God for all your needs, so that you may prosper." (Qur'an 24:30-31)

In the verse mentioned above there are many instructions for believing women.

i) Muslim women are also instructed to control their eyes, protect their private parts and guard their chastity. Thus these instructions are common for both men and women. But for women there are additional guidelines.

ii) Women are asked to cover themselves properly so that their charms and adornments are not revealed and they are advised to put on dupattas, or shawls to cover upper part of their body when they are at homes.

iii) Women are also asked to walk decently and should not flaunt their charms to avoid men's undue attention. These are the preventive measures advised by God that are beneficial for both men and women.

iv) Lastly, there is a list of relatives, including servants and subordinates, where there is some relaxation in the guidelines about Dupattas keeping in view the practical problems of family life. The verse is self explanatory so there is no need of further elaboration.

- **Outer garments for women when in public.**

"O' Prophet! Tell your wives and your daughters and wives of believers that they should draw over themselves some of their outer garments (when in public), so that they are recognized and they are not harmed. God is the most Forgiving and most Merciful." (Qur'an 33:59)

The above verse directly addresses Prophet Mohammad (Pbuh), but the instructions apply to all Muslims. The women are asked to cover themselves with outer garments when they move out of house. The actual Arabic word used in the verse is 'Jalabeeb' (Jilbab- singular). It includes a shawl, a scarf, or a Burqa. The reason given in the verse is, they may be recognized and not be troubled by street urchins and rogues.

It is a common observation that when a woman moves in public wearing indecent clothes, sometimes she becomes a victim of teasing and molestation. Moreover, law enforcement agencies are not always there to protect them. So women should take precautions to avoid such undesirable things.

Some Muslim women cover their faces when they move out of house, but it is not mentioned in Quran, nor was it a practice during the lifetime of the prophet Mohammad (SAW). It entered into Muslim societies from other communities and tribes when Islam expanded outside Arabian Peninsula. As a general rule, there is no compulsion in Islam so women are free either to cover or not to cover their faces. Although the above instructions are specially given to Muslims, their benefits are universal. Non-Muslims can also benefit from these precautionary measures..

- **Seeking permission to enter bedrooms:**

"O you who believe! Permission must be requested by your servants and those of you who have not reached puberty on three occasions: before the Dawn Prayer, at noon when you change your clothes, and after the Evening Prayer. These are three occasions of privacy for you. At other times, it is not wrong for you or them to intermingle with one another. God thus clarifies the revelations for you. God is All Knowing and All Wise."

And when the children among you reach puberty, they must ask permission, as their elders used to seek permission. God thus clarifies His revelations for you. God is All Knowing and All Wise. (Q: 24: 58-59)

In the above verses, guidance is provided for all those people living together in a house. Three periods are described as private periods; before the dawn prayer, at noon, and after the evening prayer, when the adults, children, and even servants are required to obtain permission to enter the bedrooms. These are divine instructions from the All Knowing and All Wise God. Main purpose of these instructions is to take due precaution and not disturb the privacy, which may be embarrassing for all.

- **Social etiquettes:**

"Believers, do not enter the houses of the Prophet, unless you are invited for a meal. Do not linger until a meal is ready. When you are invited enter and when you have taken your meal, depart. Do not stay on, indulging in conversation. Doing that causes annoyance to the Prophet, though he is too reticent to tell you so, but God is not reticent with the truth. " (Qur'an: 33:53)

The above verse, though addressed directly to Prophet (saw) but it is applicable to everyone. These are some of the social etiquettes which we should keep in mind whenever we go to relative or a friend for meals. Neither should we go too early nor should stay for long after the meals. It may cause inconvenience to the host.

- **Curtain between ladies and gents**

"When you ask [the wives of the Prophet] for anything, ask them from behind a curtain. That will be purer for your hearts as well as their hearts. It is not right for you to cause annoyance to the Messenger of God or for you ever to marry his wives after him. Indeed that would be an enormity in the sight of God."

(Qur'an: 33: 53)

In this portion of the verse there are two commands for us. First, whenever we ask for anything from the 'namohrim' ladies we should talk to them from behind the curtain. By namohrim we mean all those persons with whom matrimonial relations can be established. For mohrim there is no such restriction. Secondly, the wives of the Prophet (saw) are the mothers of the believers.

- **Relaxation for old women about dupatta**

" For women past the age of childbearing, who have no desire for marriage, there is no wrong if they take off their outer clothing, provided they do not flaunt their adorations. But if they can restrain themselves it is better for them. And God is All Hearing and All Knowing." (Qur'an 24: 60)

In the above-mentioned verse, the old women who have crossed the age of bearing children and who have no desire of marriage are given relaxation to take off shawl or Dupatta if they feel uncomfortable but they should take care not to reveal their 'Sater'. However, if they could put on Dupatta, Allah says it is good for them.

In this way Almighty God has provided us a very comprehensive guidance regarding control over gaze, dress code, Hijab and other social etiquettes for both men and women.

==================================

CHAPTER SEVENTEEN

17. Inheritance of Property

To build a healthy society there must be well defined and equitable laws of inheritance of property. In the absence of such laws there are chances of serious disputes and infightings. For this purpose Almighty God has provided elaborate guidelines about the rights of individuals in the property in His Holy Book Qur'an. Various verses are presented under.

a. ***Share of sons and daughters:***

"***Men shall have a share in what parents and relatives leave behind, and women shall have a stake in what parents and relatives leave behind; whether it be little or much, the share is ordained. (by God)***" (Qur'an 4:7)

It means both sons and daughters have a share in the properties left by parents. Another point that we learn is that the share in the property is not restricted to only parental properties; it may extend to properties of other near relatives. It is also clarified that property distribution must be done according to the law, irrespective of the size of the property. The share of each heir is ordained by God so there shall not be any attempt to amend such instructions. A clear system of law prevents future property-related problems.

a. **The share of a son is twice that of a daughter:**

"***Concerning your children, God enjoins you that a son shall receive a share equivalent to that of two daughters. But if there are more than two daughters, their share is two-thirds of the inheritance. And if there is only one daughter, she will receive half.***" (Qur'an 4:11)

In accordance with the above verse, the son's share is twice that of a daughter. If only one son and one daughter are the legal heirs, the property should be divided into three parts. Two parts would be given to the son and one to the daughter.

And if the heirs comprise two or more daughters only, then all daughters should share equally in the two third of the property and the remaining one-third should go to both the parents to be shared equally, i.e., $1/6^{th}$ each.

However, if there is only one daughter, then she would get only half of the property. The remaining half would go to the parents of the deceased. Mother would get $1/6^{th}$ and the balance would go to father as residuary.

God, the creator of man, knows best how the property should be distributed among legal heirs keeping in view the needs and interests of family members. He did not leave this matter to the wisdom of man to decide the share because **He knew that whoever would try to make inheritance laws would not remain neutral and would not be able to do justice.** He would think of his sectarian interest first. So All-Knowing God himself framed detailed rules and gave them to humanity.

a. **Share of Parents in the property of deceased children:**

"Each of your parents receives one-sixth of what you leave if you have children. If you are childless and your heirs are your parents; then your mother receives one third. If you have brothers (or sisters) your mother receives one-sixth after the deduction of any bequest you make or the payment of any debts" (Qur'an 4:11.)

It means if a person dies and has left one or more children, then the share of each of the parents would be one-sixth. After payment of the share of parents, the balance amount would be distributed amongst the children in proportion to their share ordained by God.

If a person dies and he leaves no child or wife, then the mother's share would be 1/3 and 2/3 would go to the father as residuary. If the deceased person had brothers or sisters, then mother's share would be reduced to one-sixth. Father would get the balance as residuary. It should be remembered that brothers and sisters have no right to the property if the mother and/or father are alive. The distribution of property should be done after the payment in accordance with the will and repayment of debts outstanding, if any.

d. **Share of spouses in the Property**

'You will inherit half of what your wives leave, provided they have left no children. But if they leave children, you shall inherit a quarter of what they leave after payment of any bequests they may have made or any debts-they have incurred. And your wives shall inherit one-quarter of what

you leave if you are childless. But if you leave children your wives shall inherit one eighth after payment of any bequest or debts." (Qur'an 4:12)

The husband has a share in the property left by his wife. If she died without any child, the husband's share would be one-half, but if she left a child, the husband's share would be reduced to one-fourth.

Similarly, a wife has a share in the property left by her husband, if he were childless, the share of the wife would be one-fourth, and if he had a child, then the share of the wife in the property would be reduced to one-eighth. These shares will be distributed after payment of any amount as per the will and after the clearance of debts in the deceased husband's name.

e. **Share of Brothers and Sisters:**

'They ask you for 'Fatwa' (Legal Opinion). Say, regarding Qalalah (When a person dies without direct legal heirs), God instructs you that if a person dies childless but has a sister, she receives half of what he leaves, and he is her heir if she dies childless. If there are two sisters, they receive two-thirds of what he leaves. If there are brothers and sisters, the share of each male shall be that of two females. God makes things clear to you so that you shall not go astray. God knows all things.' (Qur'an 4:176)

It was a practice of Prophet Mohammad that he would not give any legal opinion about any matter if there were no revelation or command of Allah. The verse mentioned above is one example. When people asked him about the legal heirs of a Qalalah, that means a person who does not have any legal heirs in the first category, i.e., Parents, children, or wife at the time of his death. Prophet

Mohammad deferred the reply till he received the above verse.

Accordingly, when a man dies without leaving any direct legal heir but has a sister, she will receive half of what her brother leaves behind. But if a woman dies without any natural heir, her brother would get a full share after paying the bequest and debts. And if there are two or more sisters as legal heirs of a man, then they shall share equally in the two thirds portion. Regarding the remaining one-third, the matter may be referred to experts in jurisprudence. And if a man leaves brothers and sisters both as legal heirs, then the share of each male member shall be that of two females.

Regarding Islamic inheritance laws, some questions are raised as to why all the legal heirs are not treated equally and why the share of sisters is half that of brothers. In Qur'an, no specific reasons are given by the Creator of Human beings, but that does not mean that there are no sound reasons. God knows everything and the knowledge of man is only limited. So man should follow the command as given by his Creator.

f. **Only God is competent to frame laws of Inheritance**

"Concerning your father and your son, you do not know who out of them will benefit you more. And this fixation of shares is by God, and He is All Knowing and All-Wise!" (Qur'an 4:11)

If we go through the laws of inheritance of the property of different communities or even secular civil laws, we will find them simple and easy but they create a lot of problems in their application. In most civil laws, all the legal heirs at one level have an equal share in the property. But brothers and sisters often do not agree in an equal division of parental property. And the reason behind this dispute is that the share of sons in the creation of property is often more than that of daughters. Secondly, we know that human society is primarily patriarchal. After the marriage, the daughter leaves the parental house and resides with her husband and in-laws. So, it is mostly the sons who look after the day-to-day needs of the parents and take care of various family relations. It is also the moral responsibility of sons to take care of their parents lifelong.

Thirdly, we observe that the strength of our relationship bonds changes with the time. Take the example of a man. His relationship with his parents, brothers and sisters is powerful when he is unmarried but when he is married there is some change because now he has to take care of his wife and children also. So we can say a man can't design a just and fair law of inheritance of property for the society.

==================================

CHAPTER EIGHTEEN

18. Prophet Muhammad – the Ideal for Believers

In addition to the Quran's teachings for humanity's guidance, God appointed Muhammad (pbuh) as His messenger and role model. The life history of Prophet is preserved in the form of his biography and his sayings in the books of Hadith. Muhammad (pbuh) was not a saint or monk, but a true messenger of God, he lived in the society, faced its challenges successfully, conveyed and explained the divine commands and guidance, and demonstrated to the people how a virtuous man should live in this world. As we learn so many things from the Qur'an regarding family relations, so also we can learn several things from the life of Prophet Muhammad and be successful not only in this world but also in the Hereafter.

While reading Quran, we find many verses that deal with the life, mission, and character of Prophet (saw). Here we would like to mention a few.

- **Best role model**

"Indeed, for you and those who believe in God and the Last Day and who always remember God, there is a good

example in the life of the Prophet of God." (Qur'an 33:21)

There is a good example and role model for the believers in the life of Prophet Muhammad (PBUH). Many authentic books are available on his life in almost all major languages of the world. Not only Muslims but followers of other religions too have studied and learned important lessons from his life.

"It is He, Who has raised among the 'ummiyeen' a messenger from among themselves, who recites His revelations to them, purifies them, and teaches them the Book and wisdom, for they had been misguided earlier." (Qur'an 62:2)

During the time of Prophet (pbuh) polytheism and idol worship was widely practiced in the Arabian Peninsula. They are called as 'Ummieen' because they had lost all the teachings of Prophet Abraham and Prophet Ismail (pbut) who were their ancestors. There were some tribes of Jews and Christians but they did not have much influence in the region. Prophet (pbuh) was from the Arabian tribe called Quraish. Almighty God appointed him His Messenger when he was around forty. His mission and role is described in the verse mentioned above as 1) He recites the revelation (Qur'an) to them. 2) He purifies them. (3) He teaches them and explains to them various instructions given in Qur'an and 4) He teaches them wisdom as to how to succeed in both worlds.

- **Prophet is mentioned in the earlier holy books**

"***Those who follow the messenger - the unlettered Prophet- find him mentioned in Torah and the Gospel with them. He commands them to do right and forbids them to do wrong. He makes good things lawful to them and bad***

things unlawful. And he relieves them of their burdens and yokes that are upon them. So those who believe in him, honour him, help him, follow the light (Quran) which is sent down with him, it is they who will prosper."

(Qur'an 7:157)

In verse mentioned above covers the following points.

1. Those, who follow the Apostle of God, shall prosper. 2. The arrival of Prophet Muhammad (saw) is also mentioned in the earlier Holy Scriptures - the Torah and the Gospel. 3. He commands them to do the right things and forbids them from wrong. 4. He makes good things lawful and bad things unlawful. 5. He relieves them of the burden of bad customs, traditions, and faith. 6. Those who believe in him, help and follow him shall prosper.

- **Prophet is gentle and kind hearted**

"***It is by God's grace that you are gentle with them, for if you were harsh and hard-hearted, they would indeed have deserted you. So bear with them, pray for their forgiveness and consult them in the conduct of affairs. And when you have made a decision, trust in God. Indeed God loves those who trust him."*** (Qur'an 3:159)

In the above verse, God appreciates the quality of Muhammad (saw) that he was gentle in dealing with the people. Had he been harsh, many would have deserted him. Almighty God advised him to condone their shortcomings. He should pray to God for their forgiveness, and while taking important decisions should consult them. And once he takes a decision he should trust God and go ahead with his plan.

- **Prophet is deeply concerned about their welfare**

"There has come to you a messenger from amongst yourselves. It grieves him that you should perish. He is deeply concerned about your welfare and is full of kindness and mercy towards believers." (Qur'an 9:128)

Prophet is from their own tribe and he is deeply concerned about their fate in the Hereafter. He wished to save them from the fire of hell. Also, he was very kind and merciful towards the believers.

- **Prophet was a human being**

"Say, I am only a human being like you. It is revealed to me that your God is one God. So let him who hopes to meet his Lord do good deeds, and let him associate no one else in the worship of his Lord". (Qur'an 18:110)

In the above verse, Almighty God has asked Muhammad (saw) to declare that he is a human being and a Messenger of God. He was privileged to receive revelation from Almighty God for the guidance of humanity. Also, he was commanded to convey that there is only one God and only He should be worshipped without associating anyone with Him.

"***Say, I have no control over any harm or benefit to myself, except by the will of God***" (Qur'an 10;49)

God has asked Mohammad (saw) to clarify to the people that although he is a Messenger of God, he does not have any power to harm or benefit himself or others. All powers are with the Almighty Lord.

- **Prophet was not an angel**

"Say, I do not say to you that I possess the treasures of God, nor do I know the unseen (Ghaib) nor tell you that

I am an angel. I follow only that which is revealed to me. Say, are the blind and the seeing alike? So why can you not think?" (Qur'an 6:50)

In this verse, too, God has asked Prophet (pbuh) to clarify by his tongue that

1) Although he is the Messenger of God, he does not own the treasures of God, so people should not expect that he can bless them with wealth or children or any other gifts. 2) That he does not know the 'unseen.' By the word unseen, we mean all the things that are not visible or will occur in the future. 3) He further clarified that he is not an angel he is only a man who follows the commands of God.

- **Prophet is for whole mankind**

"We have sent you as a bearer of glad tidings and a Warner for the whole mankind, but most people do not know." (Qur'an 34:28)

Lastly, God says that Prophet Muhammad (pbuh) is for all humanity and not for the Arabs or Muslims alone. He is responsible for warning the wrongdoers and giving glad tidings to the virtuous people.

==================================

Aftab Alam Khan

Aftab Alam Khan has spent thirty four years in Bank of Maharashtra as branch manager, senior manager and senior faculty in training centre. He is M.Sc. in Chemistry and has experiance of teaching chemistry in three colleges. He is a social activist and has a passion of learning Quran and islamic literature.

The book is an attempt to present Quranic view on various issues related to family relations. It covers origin of human society, husband wife relationship, parents and child relationship, marriage and divorce, inheritance of property, hijab and divrese social relations. It will be useful for the young generation educated through english medium to learn the Quranic teachings on various family matters. It will also be benificial for those, who could not get access to the vast isalmic literature available in urdu and other regional languages.

====

www.ingramcontent.com/pod-product-compliance
Ingram Content Group UK Ltd.
Pitfield, Milton Keynes, MK11 3LW, UK
UKHW021935190726
13853UKWH00004B/1461

9 798889 356387